**Enjoy the tastes of the sea with the
St. George Island Cookbook!**

The St. George Island Cookbook is provided for use during
your stay compliments of Collins Vacation Rentals, Inc.

Please enjoy the cookbook during your stay and leave this
copy for the next guest. If you would like to purchase a copy
to take home or as a gift, please stop by one of the local
St. George Island businesses: Island Adventures,
Sometimes It's Hotter and Island Dog Beach & Surf Shop.
All proceeds from the cookbook provide funding for our St.
George Island First Responders.

A Taste of St. George Island

The Art of Gulf Coast Cooking

A Taste of St. George Island

The Art of Gulf Coast Cooking

The proceeds from the sale of *A Taste of St. George Island* will be used to benefit
the St. George Island First Responders, a unit of the St. George Island Volunteer Fire Department.
Thank you to all of our friends who contributed their recipes, their time, and their efforts,
all of which made this book possible.

Art by Beth Appleton
History by Cindy Clark

Cookbook Committee
Alice D. Collins   Judi Little   Mary Lou Short

Published by

 Favorite Recipes® Press

An imprint of

 SOUTHWESTERN Publishing Group®

P.O. Box 305142
Nashville, Tennessee 37230
1-800-358-0560

Publisher and President: Dave Kempf
Editorial Director: Mary Cummings
Art Director: Steve Newman
Project Editor: Ginger Dawson

Library of Congress Control Number: 2013907662
ISBN: 978-0-87197-592-8

This cookbook is a collection of favorite recipes, which are not necessarily original recipes.

Manufactured in the United States of America
First Printing: 2013
5,000 copies

Acknowledgments

St. George Island is a pristine barrier island located between Tallahassee and Panama City. The Island is known for its beautiful, unspoiled beaches, shimmering Gulf waters, delicious seafood, and friendly "natives."

It has been our goal to not only create a book of exceptional recipes, but to also share some of the beloved recipes of those who love St. George Island. Many of the recipes in this book have been handed down from generation to generation, friend to friend. This collection of recipes reflects the diversity and creativity of those whose recipes are found in *A Taste of St. George Island*. All are tried and true and enjoyed by Island contributors, and we sincerely appreciate each person who took the time to contribute recipes.

We are so grateful to Beth Appleton, a very talented Island artist, who has provided the stunning artwork in *A Taste of St. George Island*. Beth's collaboration in the cookbook has been invaluable. Her artwork is unique and memorable.

We are so proud of our Island and even more pleased that your generosity, through the purchases of this book, will benefit the St. George Island Volunteer First Responders, a unit of the St. George Island Volunteer Fire Department. *A Taste of St. George Island* is the fourth cookbook we have published. Our cookbooks have helped the First Responders purchase a fully equipped emergency vehicle and medical supplies for our volunteers.

Finally, we want to thank you! Without your support, all of this effort would have been in vain. It is you who will allow us to continue to meet the needs of our community with the proceeds from this book. We invite you to enjoy these recipes and we hope that you, too, will discover a little bit of Island life in *A Taste of St. George Island—The Art of Coastal Cooking*.

Alice Collins
Judi Little
Mary Lou Short

St. George Island History

St. George Island is a 22-mile barrier island that hosts some of Florida's most beautiful and serene beaches. With no high rises anywhere, SGI is an unspoiled island with a laid-back attitude. There are twenty miles of beach on the Gulf side and miles of marsh, inlets, and oyster bars on the bayside. The uncrowded beaches are perfect for sunning and shelling, the clear Gulf waters invite swimming and fishing, and the pristine bay marshes feature extraordinary wildlife and sunset viewing.

Rent a kayak, boat, bicycle, or scooter. Accommodations, which range from quaint beach cottages to luxurious beach homes, can be reserved with any of the Island's vacation rental companies. Or stay at the hotel or inn.

Pet-Friendly

St. George Island is one of the few beaches that allows pets, and many of the vacation homes are pet-friendly. Some of the restaurants permit you to dine outside with your pet.

St. George Island State Park

The St. George Island State Park occupies the far eastern end of St. George Island. There you will find nine miles of undeveloped shoreline, majestic dunes, a bay forest, and salt marshes. The park has a series of hiking trails, boardwalks, and observation platforms. And, for the past three years, the St. George Island State Park ranked among the Top 10 Beaches of America.

Birding is a popular activity on St. George Island. You might encounter one of the many migratory birds that use St. George Island as a stopover on their way south or north.

History of St. George Island

The history of St. George Island is colored with pirates, Indians, and shipwrecks. The Creek Indians first inhabited the island as early as the 1600s. The Indians were aggressive traders, and commerce flourished from the St. Marks River around and up the Apalachicola River.

The arrival of the Europeans to the island was followed by intensive struggles for control of the area. Pirate Captain William Augustus Bowles led the Creek Indians in their defense against the Spanish and French in the late 1700s. Legend has it that before Bowles died he buried a treasure somewhere on the island.

After the Forbes Purchase in 1803, commercial sailing traffic increased and a lighthouse was built on the west end of the island, which is now Little St. George Island. Following years of coastal erosion, the Cape St. George Light toppled into the Gulf in 2005. It has been rebuilt by lighthouse enthusiasts in its present location in the center of the St. George Island business district. It is the centerpiece of the Island's Lighthouse Park, along with the Keeper's Museum.

About the Artist, Beth Appleton

"It is easy to see how my art has been influenced by this amazing place," says local Island artist Beth Appleton. She and her adventure guide husband, David, have been happy to call St. George Island home for more than two decades. "The weather, sky, light, and rich diversity of life are dynamic and like the water, they all surround and inspire us."

Her love for the Island comes naturally as a third-generation native Floridian. Growing up in Ocala, she swam in crystal clear springs and lakes. Learning underwater ballet as a child, she loved synchronized swimming and dreamed of being a Weekie Wachee mermaid. Dance and creative writing would pave the way for the lyrical artworks and books she would later create. While studying art at Florida State University, Appleton discovered the Island in the 1970s and has followed her dream to establish an art studio here.

Island Girl Cut Paper Assemblage

"Artists reflect what they come in contact with; if it gets into your soul, it gets into your art."

Appleton has recently written a children's book about our area called *Gently Down the Stream*, which focuses on the importance of protecting our fragile estuary, bay, and river.

When invited to be the featured artist for our cookbook, **A Taste of St. George Island**, Appleton was pleased to accept.

"This is a fun way for all of us to help our Island First Responders. They are not just our neighbors; they are modern day heroes."

Known for her cut paper assemblages, Appleton's art is collected internationally. Now exploring the life found within a tiny drop of water, her recent works depict detailed microscopic underwater worlds.

To see more images and to contact the artist, please visit her Web site, bethappleton.net.

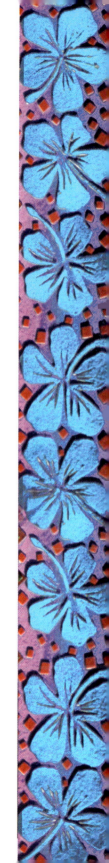

Table of Contents

Table of Contents

Rise and Shine

Aunt Pat's Egg Casserole

1 pound bulk pork sausage
Softened butter
6 slices bread
8 ounces cheese, shredded
Salt and pepper to taste
6 eggs
4 cups milk

Brown the sausage in a skillet, stirring until crumbly; drain.

Lightly butter the bread. Tear the bread into bite-size pieces and spread half over the bottom of a deep 8x8-inch baking dish.

Top with half the sausage, then sprinkle with half the cheese. Season lightly with salt and pepper. Repeat the layers with the remaining bread, sausage and cheese.

Beat the eggs in a bowl. Whisk the milk into the eggs. Pour over the layers; do not stir. Chill, covered, for 8 to 10 hours.

Bake at 350 degrees for 1 hour or until set.

Serves 8 to 10

Sausage and Egg Pie

1 (9-inch) pie pastry
4 slices mozzarella cheese
1 pound bulk pork sausage
4 eggs
3/4 cup milk
Salt and pepper to taste

Fit the pie pastry into a pie plate. Lay 2 slices of the cheese over the bottom of the pie pastry.

Brown the sausage in a skillet, stirring until crumbly; drain. Spoon the sausage into the pie pastry, then top with the remaining cheese.

Beat the eggs, milk, salt and pepper together in a bowl. Pour over the layers.

Bake at 350 degrees for 35 minutes or until set.

Serves 6 to 8

Sausage Cream Cheese Roll-Ups

1 pound bulk pork breakfast sausage
16 ounces cream cheese, softened
1/2 cup chopped red bell pepper
1/2 cup chopped green onions
2 (8-count) cans crescent roll dough

Brown the sausage in a skillet, stirring until crumbly; drain. Add the cream cheese, stirring until melted. Add the bell pepper and green onions and mix well. Cook until slightly softened.

Unroll one can of the crescent roll dough on a work surface, pressing the seams to seal. Spread half the cream cheese mixture over the dough. Roll up from the long side as for a jelly roll. Wrap tightly in plastic wrap. Repeat with the remaining crescent roll dough and cream cheese mixture.

Freeze the rolls for 2 hours or longer. Unwrap and slice into 1/2-inch pieces. Arrange on a greased baking sheet.

Bake at 375 degrees for 15 to 20 minutes or until golden brown.

Note: The rolls can be prepared and frozen for several weeks before baking. If frozen through, let thaw for 30 minutes before slicing.

Makes 40 to 50

French Toast Casserole

3/4 cup (1¹/2 sticks) butter
1¹/2 cups packed brown sugar
1¹/2 teaspoons cinnamon
1 loaf sliced whole wheat sandwich bread
6 eggs
2 cups milk
¹/2 cup maple syrup

Melt the butter with the brown sugar and cinnamon in a saucepan, stirring until of a paste consistency. Spread over the bottom of a 9×13-inch baking dish.

Trim and discard the crusts from the bread. Arrange the bread in two layers, filling in the gaps with torn pieces of bread.

Beat the eggs and milk in a bowl. Pour over the bread layers. Chill, covered, for 8 to 10 hours. Drizzle with the maple syrup.

Bake at 350 degrees for 25 to 30 minutes or until set. Broil briefly to brown the top, if desired.

Note: Be sure to use sandwich bread, not heavy whole grain bread.

Serves 8

Orange Cinnamon French Toast

2 to 4 tablespoons butter, melted
2 tablespoons (or more) honey
$^1/_2$ teaspoon cinnamon
3 eggs
$^1/_2$ cup orange juice
$^1/_8$ teaspoon salt (optional)
6 slices bread

Mix the butter, honey and cinnamon together in a bowl. Pour into a 9×13-inch baking dish and spread to coat the bottom.

Whisk the eggs, orange juice and salt in a shallow bowl. Dip both sides of each bread slice in the egg mixture and arrange in the baking dish.

Bake at 400 degrees for 15 to 20 minutes or until golden brown. Invert the French toast onto a serving platter. Drizzle with additional honey, if desired.

Serves 4 to 6

Holy Bread Pudding

4 cups cubed Hawaiian bread
$1/2$ cup raisins
8 ounces cream cheese, chopped
4 to 6 eggs
$1^1/2$ cups milk
$2/3$ cup sugar
1 tablespoon pumpkin pie spice
1 teaspoon vanilla extract
$1/2$ cup (1 stick) butter, melted

Layer the bread, raisins and cream cheese in a 9×13-inch baking dish.

Combine the eggs, milk, sugar, pumpkin pie spice and vanilla in a blender and process until combined. Pour over the layers. Drizzle the butter over the top.

Let stand for 1 hour or chill, covered, for 8 to 10 hours.

Bake at 350 degrees for 40 minutes or until set. Serve with maple syrup.

Note: You may substitute 1 cup fresh berries and 1 teaspoon almond extract for the cream cheese and pumpkin pie spice.

Serves 8

Easy Cheese Danish

16 ounces cream cheese, softened
1/2 to 1 cup sugar
2 tablespoons lemon juice
1 egg yolk
1 teaspoon vanilla extract
2 (8-count) cans crescent roll dough
1 egg white

Beat the cream cheese, sugar, lemon juice, egg yolk and vanilla in a bowl until blended.

Unroll one can of the crescent roll dough over the bottom of a baking dish, pressing the seams to seal. Spoon the cream cheese mixture evenly over the dough.

Unroll the remaining can of dough on a work surface, pressing the seams to seal. Arrange over the top of the cream cheese mixture. Brush with the egg white.

Bake at 350 degrees for 30 to 35 minutes or until the top is light brown.

Serves 10 to 15

Praline-Topped Apple Bread

1 cup granulated sugar
1 cup sour cream
2 eggs
1 tablespoon vanilla extract
2 cups all-purpose flour
2 teaspoons baking powder
1/2 teaspoon baking soda
11/2 cups chopped peeled Granny Smith apples
1 cup chopped pecans, toasted
1/2 cup (1 stick) butter
1/2 cup packed brown sugar
1/4 cup chopped pecans, toasted

Beat the granulated sugar, sour cream, eggs and vanilla in a bowl. Combine the flour, baking powder and baking soda in a bowl. Stir into the sour cream mixture just until moistened. Fold in the apples and 1 cup pecans. Spoon into a greased 5×9-inch loaf pan.

Bake at 350 degrees for 50 to 55 minutes or until the loaf tests done. Cool in the pan for 10 minutes. Remove to a wire rack to cool completely.

Melt the butter and brown sugar in a saucepan. Bring to a boil and boil for 1 minute, stirring constantly. Pour over the bread. Sprinkle with ¼ cup pecans.

Serves 15

Apricot Bread

1/2 cup dried apricots, chopped
1/4 cup water
1 egg
1 cup granulated sugar
2 teaspoons butter, melted
2 cups all-purpose flour
2 teaspoons baking powder

11/2 teaspoons baking soda
1/2 teaspoon salt
1/2 cup strained orange juice
1 teaspoon grated orange zest
1 cup chopped pecans
Additional orange juice
Confectioners' sugar

Soak the apricots in the water in a small bowl for 30 minutes; drain. Beat the egg in a large bowl. Stir in the granulated sugar and butter. Mix the flour, baking powder, baking soda and salt together. Add to the egg mixture alternately with 1/2 cup orange juice. Stir in the orange zest. Stir in the apricots and pecans. Pour into a greased and floured loaf pan.

Bake at 350 degrees for 1 hour or until a toothpick inserted into the center comes out clean. Let cool slightly, then remove from the pan to cool completely.

Whisk a small amount of orange juice with confectioners' sugar in a bowl until of a glaze consistency. Drizzle over the bread.

Serves 6 to 8

Beer Bread

3 cups self-rising flour
3 tablespoons sugar
12 ounces beer
2 tablespoons butter, melted

Sift the flour and sugar together into a bowl. Add the beer, stirring just until a few lumps remain; the batter will be thick. Pour into a greased loaf pan.

Bake at 350 degrees for 50 minutes. Pour the butter over the top and bake for 10 minutes longer.

Note: The type of beer used will affect the flavor of the bread. Light beer will make sweeter bread, while a darker beer will yield a heartier taste.

Serves 8 to 10

Sand Dunes

Beaches and sand dunes confront tremendous energies from storm waves, tides, and winds. They act as shock absorbers to protect the coastal environment. Dunes accumulate sand in normal conditions and release it to the beach during major storms. This sand reserve helps beaches resist wave energy and provides material to help rebuild the beaches after storms. Protected by Florida law, the most prolific and valuable dune vegetation is the sea oat.

19

Broccoli Corn Bread

1 (8-ounce) package corn bread mix
4 eggs
1/2 cup (1 stick) butter, softened
3/4 cup cottage cheese
1/2 teaspoon salt
1 (10-ounce) package frozen
chopped broccoli, thawed
1 large onion, chopped

Combine the corn bread mix, eggs, butter, cottage cheese and salt in a large bowl. Stir in the broccoli and onion. Pour into a 9×9-inch baking pan.
Bake at 375 to 400 degrees for 20 to 30 minutes or until light golden brown.

Serves 8

How to Find a Sand Dollar

*Sand dollars can be found on the beaches and the shallow sand flats.
The best time to find them is at low tide or after a storm.
Wade in, ankle to waist deep, across the sand bottom. Look for the top of
a sand dollar just protruding from the sand. Carefully gather the sand dollar
and place it in a flat bucket. To clean your sand dollars,
place in a solution of 50 percent bleach and 50 percent water. Soak until
they turn white. Rinse with fresh water and let dry in the sun.*

Dilly Bread

2 envelopes dry yeast
$1/2$ cup warm water
2 cups cottage cheese
2 extra-large eggs, lightly beaten
$1/4$ cup sugar
$1/4$ cup dill seeds
2 tablespoons butter, softened
2 tablespoons minced onion
2 teaspoons salt
$1/2$ teaspoon baking soda
Melted butter
Salt to taste

Combine the yeast and water in a small bowl; set aside. Spoon the cottage cheese into a microwave-safe bowl and warm slightly in the microwave. Stir in the eggs, sugar, dill seeds, 2 tablespoons butter, onion, 2 teaspoons salt and baking soda. Stir in the yeast mixture. Pour into a greased 5×8-inch loaf pan and let rise for 1 hour.

Bake at 350 degrees for 30 to 35 minutes or until the bread tests done. Remove to a wire rack to cool. Brush with melted butter and sprinkle with salt.

Serves 8 to 10

Strawberry Bread with Spread

2 (10-ounce) packages frozen strawberries, thawed
3 cups all-purpose flour
2 cups sugar
1 teaspoon cinnamon
1 teaspoon baking powder
1 teaspoon salt
1 1/4 cups vegetable oil
4 eggs, beaten
1 cup chopped pecans
8 ounces cream cheese, softened

Slice the strawberries, reserving 1/2 cup of the juice. Combine the flour, sugar, cinnamon, baking powder and salt in a bowl. Make a well in the center of the dry ingredients. Add the strawberries, oil and eggs to the well and mix well. Stir in the pecans. Pour the batter evenly into two greased and floured loaf pans.

Bake at 350 degrees for 45 to 60 minutes or until the bread tests done.

Combine the reserved 1/2 cup strawberry juice with the cream cheese in a blender. Process until of spreading consistency. Slice the bread and serve with the strawberry spread.

Serves 12

Easy Pecan Rolls

1 tablespoon butter
1/2 cup chopped pecans
2 (12-count) packages frozen dinner rolls
1 (4-ounce) package butterscotch cook-and-serve pudding mix
7 tablespoons butter, melted
1/2 cup packed brown sugar
1/4 teaspoon cinnamon

Coat the bottom of a 9x13-inch baking pan with 1 tablespoon butter. Sprinkle the pecans over the butter. Arrange the rolls over the pecans and sprinkle with the pudding mix.

Combine 7 tablespoons melted butter with the brown sugar and cinnamon in a bowl and mix well. Pour over the rolls. Let rise, uncovered, for 6 to 10 hours.

Bake at 350 degrees for 30 minutes. Invert the rolls onto a serving tray immediately.

Serves 12

Butterhorn Yeast Rolls

2 envelopes dry yeast
1/4 cup warm water
1 cup scalded milk
1/2 cup (1 stick) butter or shortening
1/2 cup sugar
1 teaspoon salt
3 eggs, beaten
4 1/2 cups all-purpose flour

Stir the yeast into the warm water in a cup. Let stand until bubbly. Mix the milk, butter, sugar and salt in a saucepan and heat through. Let cool to lukewarm. Stir in the yeast mixture. Mix in the eggs. Mix in the flour until a smooth dough forms.

Knead lightly on a floured work surface. Place in a greased bowl and let rise, covered, until doubled in size.

Divide the dough into three portions. Roll each portion into a 9-inch circle on a floured surface. Cut each into three or four wedges. Roll up each wedge starting at the wide end. Arrange the rolls point side down on a baking sheet.

Bake at 375 degrees for 12 to 15 minutes or until light brown.

Serves 12 to 16

Banana Bread Muffins

1 cup sugar
$1/2$ cup vegetable oil
1 medium egg
$1/2$ teaspoon vanilla extract
3 ripe bananas, mashed
$1/4$ cup chopped walnuts
2 cups all-purpose flour
1 teaspoon baking soda
$1/2$ teaspoon salt

Line muffin cups with paper liners or coat with butter. Mix the sugar, oil, egg and vanilla in a bowl until creamy and light yellow. Stir in the bananas and walnuts. Add the flour, baking soda and salt and stir until smooth. Spoon into the prepared muffin cups. Bake at 350 degrees for 30 to 40 minutes or until a wooden pick inserted into the center muffin comes out clean.

Makes 1 dozen

It's Island Time!

Dina's Bruschetta

2 (15-ounce) cans diced tomatoes,
drained and rinsed
1 package fresh small mozzarella balls
4 to 6 garlic cloves, crushed
Handful of fresh basil leaves

1/3 cup olive oil
1 teaspoon (or more) balsamic vinegar
Salt and pepper to taste
1 loaf French bread, sliced

Combine the tomatoes, cheese, garlic and basil in a bowl. Stir in the olive oil and vinegar and season with salt and pepper. Chill, covered, for 2 hours or longer. Toast the bread, if desired. Spoon the bruschetta topping onto the bread slices and serve.

Serves 8 to 10

Cheese Wafers

1 cup (2 sticks) margarine, softened
8 to 10 ounces sharp Cheddar cheese,
shredded
2 cups all-purpose flour

1/8 teaspoon red pepper
1 cup crisp rice cereal
1 cup Grape-Nuts cereal

Beat the margarine in a bowl until smooth and creamy. Add the cheese and beat well. Mix the flour and red pepper together. Add to the cheese mixture and mix well. Beat in the cereal. Roll into small balls and arrange on an ungreased baking sheet. Press each ball with a fork to flatten slightly. Bake at 375 degrees for 8 to 10 minutes or until light brown.

Makes 75 wafers

Mediterranean Marinated Olives

1 teaspoon fennel seeds
1/2 teaspoon cumin seeds
1 cup black olives, pitted
1 cup green olives, pitted
2 tablespoons extra-virgin olive oil
1 tablespoon lemon juice
1 tablespoon red wine vinegar
2 garlic cloves, finely chopped
1 teaspoon crushed red pepper flakes
1 teaspoon dried oregano
Grated zest of 1/2 orange
Grated zest of 1/2 lemon

Toast the fennel and cumin seeds in a small sauté pan over low heat for
2 minutes, watching carefully to prevent overbrowning. Combine the toasted seeds,
olives, olive oil, lemon juice, vinegar, garlic, red pepper flakes, oregano, orange
zest and lemon zest in a large bowl. Toss to coat well. Pour into a container with a
tight-fitting lid. Marinate, tightly covered, at room temperature for 8 hours. Shake
occasionally to distribute the flavors. Serve at room temperature. May be prepared
ahead and stored in an airtight container in the refrigerator for up to 1 week.

Makes about 2 cups

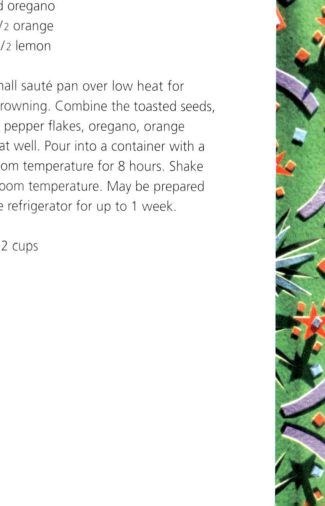

Sausage-Stuffed Jalapeño Chiles

1 pound bulk pork sausage
8 ounces cream cheese, softened

4 ounces Parmesan cheese, shredded
20 large jalapeño chiles

Brown the sausage in a large skillet, stirring until crumbly; drain. Combine the cream cheese and Parmesan cheese in a mixing bowl and beat until blended. Fold in the sausage. Cut each jalapeño lengthwise into halves and discard the seeds. Spoon about 1 tablespoon of the sausage mixture into each jalapeño half and arrange on a baking sheet. Bake at 425 degrees for 15 to 20 minutes or until the filling is light brown and bubbly. Serve with ranch dressing for dipping, if desired.

Serves 10

Roasted Pear and Goat Cheese Quesadilla

2 large pears
1 tablespoon olive oil
2 onions, thinly sliced

1 tablespoon olive oil
4 (8-inch) flour tortillas
4 ounces goat cheese

Core and slice the pears. Sauté in 1 tablespoon olive oil in a small sauté pan over medium heat for 15 minutes or until softened. Sauté the onions in 1 tablespoon olive oil in a sauté pan over low heat until softened and golden brown. Warm the tortillas in a skillet. Spread the goat cheese evenly on one side of each tortilla. Arrange the pears and onions evenly over the goat cheese on two of the tortillas. Top each with one of the remaining tortillas cheese side down. Cut into quarters and serve.

Serves 4

Bean Dip

1 (15-ounce) can pinto beans,
drained and rinsed
1 (15-ounce) can black-eyed peas,
drained and rinsed
1 (11-ounce) can Shoe Peg corn
1 small red or green bell pepper, finely chopped
1/2 small red onion, finely chopped
2 ribs celery, chopped
1/2 cup canola oil
1/2 cup olive oil
1/2 cup apple cider vinegar
1/2 cup sugar
Chopped fresh parsley (optional)

Mix the beans, black-eyed peas, corn, bell pepper, onion and celery together in a bowl. Combine the canola oil, olive oil, vinegar and sugar in a small saucepan. Cook over low heat until the sugar dissolves, stirring occasionally. Pour over the bean mixture and stir to coat well. Serve immediately or chill, covered, for 8 to 10 hours for the best results. Stir in parsley just before serving.

Serves 8

Broccoli Cheese Dip

2 (10-ounce) packages frozen
chopped broccoli
1 small onion, chopped
1 jar sliced mushrooms
1/2 cup (1 stick) butter, melted
16 ounces Velveeta cheese, chopped
1 (10-ounce) can cream of
mushroom soup
Garlic salt to taste
1 teaspoon Worcestershire sauce
Salt and pepper to taste

Prepare the broccoli according to the package directions; drain. Sauté the onion and mushrooms in the butter in a sauté pan. Microwave the cheese in a large microwave-safe bowl until melted. Stir in the soup and garlic salt. Stir in the broccoli, onion mixture, Worcestershire sauce, salt and pepper. Spoon into a fondue pot or chafing dish. Serve warm with tortilla chips.

Serves 8 to 10

Hot Clam and Cheese Dip

1/2 cup chopped onion
1 cup chopped mixed red, yellow and green bell peppers
9 tablespoons butter, melted
15 ounces chopped clams, drained
16 ounces sharp Cheddar cheese, chopped
3/4 cup ketchup
3 tablespoons Worcestershire sauce
1/2 teaspoon (or more) cayenne pepper

Sauté the onion and bell peppers in the butter in a large sauté pan until softened. Stir in the clams, cheese, ketchup, Worcestershire sauce and cayenne pepper. Cook until the cheese melts, stirring frequently. Spoon into a chafing dish. Serve warm with scoop-style tortilla chips. Reserve the clam juice for chowder or clam sauce for pasta, if desired.

Serves 8 to 10

Cathy's Crab Dip

1/2 (10-ounce) can cream of
mushroom soup
8 ounces cream cheese
1/2 cup mayonnaise-type salad dressing

1 cup chopped celery
1/4 cup minced green onions
Hot sauce to taste
2 cups lump crab meat, flaked

Heat the soup and cream cheese in a saucepan over low heat until the cheese is melted, stirring frequently. Combine with the salad dressing, celery, green onions and hot sauce in a serving bowl and mix well. Fold in the crab meat. Serve warm with crackers.

Note: The dip also makes an excellent filling for crab quesadillas.

Serves 14

Corn and Feta Dip

1/4 cup olive oil
1/4 cup apple cider vinegar
1/4 cup sugar
1 (15-ounce) can sweet corn, drained

1 (15-ounce) can black beans,
drained and rinsed
1 cup chopped sweet onion
1 cup crumbled feta cheese

Whisk the olive oil, vinegar and sugar together in a bowl until the sugar dissolves. Add the corn, beans, onion and cheese and mix well. Serve with corn chips.

Makes about 2 cups

Middle Eastern Hummus

1 (15-ounce) can chick-peas
3/4 cup tahini paste
Juice of 2 small lemons, or equivalent amount of
frozen lemon juice concentrate
1 to 3 garlic cloves
1 to 3 tablespoons olive oil
1 or 2 dashes of cayenne pepper

Drain the chick-peas, reserving 1/4 cup of the liquid. Measure 1 cup of the chick-peas, reserving any extra for another purpose. Combine the chick-peas, tahini paste, lemon juice and garlic in a food processor or blender. Process until combined. Drizzle the olive oil and reserved liquid into the food processor while running until of the desired consistency. Pour into a bowl and sprinkle with the cayenne pepper. If serving hummus as a dip, it should have a consistency similar to guacamole. If using the hummus as a spread, the consistency should be even thicker.

Serve as a dip with pita wedges, fresh vegetables and/or crackers. For a sandwich, spread the hummus on pita bread or a baguette and top with cucumber slices, lettuce and other fresh vegetables of your choice.

Serves 4 to 6

Creole Seafood Cocktail Sauce

*John B. Spohrer, Jr., makes Creole Seafood Cocktail Sauce to serve
with oysters, shrimp, or crawfish by combining 1 cup ketchup,
1 tablespoon horseradish, 1 tablespoon Worcestershire sauce,
1 teaspoon hot sauce, 1/2 cup minced celery and salt to taste.*

Smoked Fish Spread

8 ounces cream cheese, softened
1/4 cup mayonnaise
1/4 cup sour cream
1 tablespoon grated onion
1 tablespoon fresh lemon juice
1/4 teaspoon cayenne pepper
Salt and black pepper to taste
Hot sauce to taste
4 ounces smoked mullet or other smoked fish, flaked

Combine the cream cheese, mayonnaise, sour cream, onion, lemon juice, cayenne pepper, salt, black pepper and hot sauce in a bowl and mix well. Fold in the fish. Spoon into a small bowl lined with plastic wrap and chill for 2 hours or longer. Invert onto a serving plate and remove the plastic wrap. Serve with crackers.

Serves 8

The Brown Pelican

The best fisherman in the world! Not long ago, the pelican population dwindled to a handful due to pesticides, but today the pelican population is healthy and increasing in numbers. An incredible sight is to watch a pelican "dive bomb" and hit the water with a great impact. The pelican has a special air sac under the flesh on the front of the body to cushion it from the constant pounding against the water surface. The pelican does not spear its catch, but uses its pouch much like a fish net.

36

Blue Cheese Oysters

8 large oysters on the half shell
1/2 cup crumbled blue cheese
1/4 cup panko (Japanese bread crumbs)
2 tablespoons unsalted butter, softened
1 teaspoon fresh tarragon leaves, minced
1 garlic clove, chopped

Arrange the oysters on a baking sheet. Combine the cheese, bread crumbs, butter, tarragon and garlic in a small bowl and mix well. Spoon evenly over the oysters. Bake at 350 degrees for 12 minutes or until the topping bubbles and begins to brown.

Serves 4

Oysters St. George

24 large oysters on the half shell
12 saltine crackers, crushed
1/2 cup (2 ounces) shredded Cheddar cheese
2 tablespoons butter, melted
Juice of 1/2 large lemon
3 or 4 drops good-quality hot sauce, or to taste
1 garlic clove, minced
Salt and pepper to taste

Arrange the oysters on a rimmed baking sheet. Combine the cracker crumbs, cheese, butter, lemon juice, hot sauce, garlic, salt and pepper in a bowl and mix well. Spoon evenly over the oysters. Bake at 350 degrees for 7 to 10 minutes or until the topping is golden brown.

Serves 6

Lana's Baked Oysters

1 pint oysters	Shredded sharp Cheddar cheese to taste
Olive oil	Grated Parmesan cheese to taste
Jarred minced jalapeño chiles to taste	Italian bread crumbs to taste
Bacon bits to taste	

Shuck the oysters, reserving the shells. Scrub the shells, then brush the inside with olive oil. Place 1 or 2 oysters in each oyster shell and arrange on a foil-lined baking sheet. Top each oyster with 2 or 3 pieces of jalapeño. Layer the bacon bits, Cheddar cheese, Parmesan cheese and bread crumbs over the top in the order listed. Bake at 450 degrees for 5 minutes or until light brown. Serve hot, plain or with saltine crackers and/or hot sauce.

Serves 8 to 10

Oystering—Apalachicola Bay Style

Driving across the causeway, it is enchanting to see hundreds of oyster boats, or Lolly boats as they are sometimes called, dotting the bay. Oystermen typically go out early in the morning. Besides the oyster tongs, other essentials are a culling iron, culling board, and drag anchor. As oysters are brought up, they are deposited on the culling board, which extends across the boat. After the culling board is full, the tonger, using the iron, breaks off the extraneous material and small oysters, and then the culled matter is returned to the water. Tongs are long, double-handled rakes. The oysterman reaches nine or more feet into the water, scrapes shells from the beds, and brings the oysters to the surface. Tonging is laborious but remains an art.

Easy Oyster Appetizer

1 pint oysters
Garlic salt to taste
Grated Parmesan cheese to taste
Italian bread crumbs to taste

Partially drain the oysters and arrange in a single layer in a shallow 9×10-inch baking dish. Top with the garlic salt, cheese and bread crumbs. Bake at 450 degrees for 5 minutes or until light brown. Serve with saltine crackers and hot sauce.

Serves 8 to 10

Marinated Shrimp

5 pounds peeled cooked shrimp
4 red or sweet onions, thinly sliced
4 lemons, thinly sliced
4 tomatoes, peeled and chopped
1 cup olive oil
1/4 cup balsamic or apple cider vinegar
1/4 cup capers

2 garlic cloves, minced
1 tablespoon Worcestershire sauce
1 tablespoon sugar
2 teaspoons salt
1/2 teaspoon celery salt
1/2 teaspoon pepper

Layer the shrimp, onions and lemons alternately in a large container with a lid. Combine the tomatoes, olive oil, vinegar, capers, garlic, Worcestershire sauce, sugar, salt, celery salt and pepper in a bowl and mix well. Pour over the layers. Chill, covered, for 8 hours, stirring occasionally. Spoon into a serving bowl and serve cold.

Serves 10

Cheese-Stuffed Shrimp

12 large shrimp	12 slices bacon
3 slices manchego cheese, cut into strips	1 teaspoon garlic salt

Peel and devein the shrimp, leaving the tails intact. Cut a slit into each shrimp. Insert a strip of the cheese into each shrimp and wrap with a slice of bacon. Sprinkle with the garlic salt. Thread the shrimp onto skewers and arrange on a baking sheet. Bake at 350 degrees until the bacon is cooked through, turning the skewers halfway through the process. Serve hot. If preferred, the skewers may be grilled.

Notes: To serve as an entrée, double the ingredient amounts and prepare as directed above.

Serves 3 or 4

Layered Seafood Spread

16 ounces cream cheese, softened	3/4 cup chopped tomato
2 tablespoons mayonnaise	1 pound chopped cooked shrimp
2 tablespoons Old Bay seasoning	or crab meat
1/2 cup sliced green onions	

Beat the cream cheese, mayonnaise and Old Bay seasoning in a bowl until smooth and creamy. Spread evenly over a 12-inch serving platter. Sprinkle the green onions and tomato over the cream cheese layer. Top with the shrimp. Serve with crackers and/or tortilla chips.

Serves 10

Grilled Chicken Livers

1/2 cup (1 stick) unsalted butter
4 chicken bouillon cubes
Juice of 1 lemon
4 garlic cloves, minced

2 tablespoons dark brown sugar
2 teaspoons salt, or to taste
8 ounces thick-cut bacon
1 pound chicken livers

Melt the butter in a saucepan. Add the bouillon cubes and stir until dissolved. Stir in the lemon juice, garlic, brown sugar and salt. Cut each slice of bacon into halves or thirds. Wrap each chicken liver in a piece of bacon, securing with a wooden pick. Drizzle a few drops of the butter mixture onto each wrapped liver. Grill over medium heat until the bacon is cooked through, basting occasionally with the remaining butter mixture. Serve hot.

Serves 8

Mojito

6 large mint leaves
Juice of 1/2 large lime
1 ounce simple syrup

1 drop of bitters
2 to 3 ounces white rum
Splash of club soda

Muddle the mint with the lime juice in a tall 10- to 12-ounce glass. Add enough of the simple syrup to cover the mint leaves. Add the bitters. Fill the glass with ice. Add enough rum to almost fill the glass. Pour into a cocktail shaker and shake vigorously for 10 seconds. Pour back into the glass with the ice and add the club soda.

Serves 1

Chocolate Eggnog

Egg Mixture
12 egg whites
1/2 cup sugar
12 egg yolks
1 cup sugar
3/4 teaspoon salt

Eggnog
1 quart (4 cups) heavy cream, whipped
1 quart (4 cups) chocolate milk
4 cups bourbon
1 cup brandy
1 cup rum
Nutmeg to taste

For the egg mixture, beat the egg whites in a medium bowl until stiff. Beat in 1/2 cup sugar until stiff peaks form. Beat the egg yolks, 1 cup sugar and salt in a large bowl until very light. Fold in the egg whites.

For the eggnog, mix the whipped cream, chocolate milk, bourbon and brandy in a large bowl. Stir in the rum. Fold in the egg mixture. Store in 1-gallon containers for at least 1 week before serving. Ladle into mugs and sprinkle with nutmeg.

Serves 16

Fruit Tea Punch

4 cups water	1 cup orange juice
4 tea bags	4 cups water
1 cinnamon stick	8 slices lemon
3/4 cup sugar	8 sprigs of mint

Bring 4 cups water to a boil in a medium saucepan; remove from the heat. Add the tea bags and cinnamon stick and let stand, covered, for 5 minutes. Remove the tea bags. Stir in the sugar until dissolved. Stir in the orange juice. Pour into a pitcher. Add 4 cups water and mix well. Add the lemon slices and mint. Chill until cold. Discard the cinnamon stick before serving. Serve over ice in tall glasses.

Serves 8

Hot Cider Punch

1 gallon (16 cups) apple cider	1 tablespoon ground nutmeg
2 cups water	1 tablespoon ground ginger
6 whole cloves	1 cup packed brown sugar
6 whole allspice	2 cups granulated sugar
2 cinnamon sticks	

Combine the cider, water, cloves, allspice, cinnamon sticks, nutmeg and ginger in a large saucepan. Cover and bring to a boil. Boil for 10 minutes. Add the brown sugar and granulated sugar. Simmer over low heat for 15 to 30 minutes, stirring frequently. Strain, removing the spices, and serve hot in mugs.

Makes about 5 quarts

43

Sun, Soup, and Salad

Black Bean Soup

1 cup dried black beans
1 onion, chopped
1 green bell pepper, chopped
1 rib celery, chopped
1 carrot, chopped
2 garlic cloves, chopped
3 tablespoons olive oil
2 cups chicken stock
Salt and pepper to taste
1 tablespoon lemon juice

Soak the beans in cold water to cover in a stockpot for 8 to 10 hours; drain. Add fresh water to cover. Simmer for 2 hours or until almost tender.

Sauté the onion, bell pepper, celery, carrot and garlic in the olive oil in a small saucepan until almost tender. Add the sautéed vegetables and stock to the beans and simmer over medium heat until the beans are tender. Remove from the heat and let cool slightly.

Purée the soup in batches in a blender until of the desired consistency. Return to the stockpot and season with salt and pepper. Stir in the lemon juice. Cook until heated through.

Serves 12

Quick-and-Easy Bean and Spinach Soup

2¹/₂ cups chicken broth
2 cups water
4 cups trimmed baby spinach leaves
2 (16-ounce) cans cannellini beans, drained and rinsed
1 pound kielbasa, turkey kielbasa or smoked sausage links, chopped
2 potatoes or parsnips, chopped
1 onion, chopped
2 teaspoons (about) chopped fresh basil
1 teaspoon chopped garlic
1 teaspoon lemon pepper
Sour cream (optional)

Combine the broth, water, spinach, beans, sausage, potatoes and onion in a stockpot. Stir in the basil, garlic and lemon pepper and bring to a boil.

Reduce the heat and simmer, covered, for 10 minutes or until the potatoes are tender. Serve hot in bowls topped with a dollop of sour cream.

Serves 4 to 6

Cheese Soup

1/4 cup (1/2 stick) butter
3 green onions, chopped
3 ribs celery with leaves, chopped
2 carrots, finely chopped
2 cups chicken broth
8 ounces Velveeta cheese, shredded
Parsley to taste
Tabasco sauce to taste
Minced garlic to taste
Pepper to taste
1 cup milk
2 (4-ounce) packages instant mashed potatoes
1 to 2 cups chopped cooked chicken or pork

Melt the butter in a stockpot. Add the green onions, celery and carrots and cook for 5 minutes. Stir in the broth. Simmer, covered, for 30 minutes. Add the cheese, parsley, Tabasco sauce, garlic and pepper and mix well.

Cook until the cheese melts, stirring occasionally. Add the milk and instant potato flakes and cook until thickened, stirring frequently. Simmer for 15 minutes longer.

Serves 8

Sandy Mitchem's First Place Slow-Cooker Chili

1 large red onion, finely chopped
5 tablespoons olive oil
3 pounds ground organic turkey
3 (15-ounce) cans chili beans
3 cups tomato bruschetta topping
2 cups mild fresh salsa
1 (10-ounce) jar classic
   marinara sauce
1 cup lambrusco
5 tablespoons chopped
   fresh garlic
2 envelopes mild chili
   seasoning mix

1 teaspoon finely chopped
   red chiles
1 teaspoon hot sauce
Salt and pepper to taste
1¹/₂ cups (6 ounces) shredded
   Cheddar cheese
1 quart cherry tomatoes,
   cut into halves
1 large sprig of basil, leaves
   chopped
1 (7-ounce) Hershey's chocolate
   Kiss or 7 ounces Hershey's
   chocolate kisses candies

Brown the onion in the olive oil in a saucepan. Combine with the turkey, beans, bruschetta topping, salsa, marinara sauce, wine, garlic, chili seasoning mix, red chiles, hot sauce, salt and pepper in a slow cooker and mix well. Cook on Low until the turkey is cooked through and the chili is hot. Stir in the cheese, cherry tomatoes, basil and candy. Cook for 20 minutes longer. Enjoy and don't forget to add the chocolate!

Note: Since this is an award-winning recipe, you can duplicate the original recipe taste exactly by using the following brands that Sandy used, instead of your favorites: Carbonell Olive Oil; McCormick Mild Chili Seasoning Mix; Bush's Chili Beans; 3 cups (two 12-ounce jars) Bella-Famiglia Tomatoes Bruschett; Cugino's Classic Marinara!; Riunite Lambrusco wine; and Crystal Hot Sauce.

Makes about 2 quarts

Louisiana Potato-Shrimp Soup

1 package crab boil seasoning
1 quart (4 cups) water
2 potatoes, chopped into 1/2-inch pieces
1 pound medium shrimp
8 ounces cream cheese, softened
1/2 cup (1 stick) butter
1 bunch green onions, chopped
1 garlic clove, minced, or garlic powder to taste
2 cups milk
2 (10-ounce) cans potato soup
2 (15-ounce) cans whole kernel corn
2 (15-ounce) cans cream-style corn
Creole seasoning to taste

Combine the crab boil and water in a stockpot. Add the potatoes and bring to a boil. Boil for 5 minutes. Remove the potatoes to a bowl using a slotted spoon. Return the reserved cooking liquid to a boil. Add the shrimp and boil for 1 minute; drain.

Combine the cream cheese and half the butter in a microwave-safe bowl. Microwave on High until soft, then whisk together.

Melt the remaining butter in a stockpot. Add the green onions and garlic and sauté until translucent; do not overcook. Stir in the milk, potato soup and corn. Season with Creole seasoning. Bring to a simmer. Stir in the cream cheese mixture, potatoes and shrimp. Simmer until heated through. Serve with salad and toasted breadsticks.

Note: The soup can be made 1 day in advance and reheated before serving.

Serves 8

Seafood Chowder

1/2 cup (1 stick) butter
7 ounces all-purpose flour
4 cups canned chopped sea clams in liquor
4 slices bacon, crisp-cooked and crumbled
3/4 cup chopped carrots
3/4 cup chopped celery
3/4 cup chopped onion
4 cups water
4 cups heavy cream
5 large potatoes, peeled and chopped
1 pound grouper, chopped
1 pound shrimp, peeled and deveined
Salt, pepper and thyme to taste

Melt the butter in a small saucepan. Whisk in the flour gradually. Cook until thickened and smooth, stirring constantly. Set the roux aside. Drain the clams, reserving the liquor.

Combine the clams, bacon, carrots, celery and onion in a heavy stockpot. Cook until the vegetables are softened. Stir in the roux. Whisk in the water, cream and reserved clam liquor.

Cook over medium heat until thickened, stirring occasionally. Stir in the potatoes, grouper and shrimp.

Cook until the shrimp turn pink and the grouper is cooked through. Season with salt, pepper and thyme. Serve hot in bowls with warm French bread.

Serves 8

Southwestern Soup

1 pound ground chuck
1 large onion, chopped
2 garlic cloves, minced
1 (16-ounce) can light red kidney
beans, drained and rinsed
1 (16-ounce) can black beans, drained and rinsed
1 (14-ounce can) tomatoes with
jalapeño chiles
1 (14-ounce) can tomatoes with green chiles
1 (16-ounce) package frozen white corn
1 (14-ounce) can beef broth
1 envelope taco seasoning mix
1 teaspoon salt
1/2 teaspoon pepper
4 cups water
2 tablespoons chopped fresh cilantro
Tortilla chips
Shredded cheese

Brown the ground chuck with the onion and garlic in a large stockpot, stirring until crumbly; drain. Stir in the kidney beans, black beans, tomatoes, corn, broth, seasoning mix, salt, pepper and water.

Bring to a boil. Reduce the heat and simmer, covered, for 30 minutes. Stir in the cilantro just before serving.

Crumble tortilla chips into each bowl. Ladle the soup over the chips and top with cheese to serve.

Serves 12

Squash Bisque

¹/2 cup chopped onion
¹/4 cup chopped celery
1 to 1¹/2 tablespoons butter
2 cups chopped peeled butternut squash
1 potato, peeled and chopped
2 cups chicken stock
¹/2 cup light cream or half-and-half
Salt and freshly ground pepper to taste
Additional butter
Chopped fresh parsley

Sauté the onion and celery in the butter in a large saucepan until softened.
Stir in the squash, potato and stock; bring to a boil. Reduce the heat.

Simmer, covered, for 25 minutes or until the vegetables are very tender.

Pass the soup through a food mill or purée in a blender until smooth. Return to the saucepan and stir in the cream.

Cook until heated through. Season with salt and pepper. Ladle into soup bowls. Top each serving with a small slice of butter and sprinkle with chopped parsley

Serves 4

Tomato Bisque

1 (28-ounce) can crushed tomatoes,
or 28 ounces chopped peeled fresh tomatoes
2 cups water
2 tablespoons chopped onion
2 tablespoons sugar
1 teaspoon salt
1 teaspoon black pepper
Pinch of white pepper
Pinch of cayenne pepper
Sprig of fresh basil
Sprig of fresh oregano
2 cups half-and-half

Combine the tomatoes, water, onion, sugar, salt, black pepper, white pepper, cayenne pepper, basil and oregano in a large saucepan.

Cook over medium-low heat for 30 to 45 minutes or until the tomatoes are softened and the soup is heated through. Remove the basil and oregano.

Purée the soup with an immersion blender or in batches in a blender until smooth. Strain the purée, discarding any solids.

Return the soup to the saucepan and stir in the half-and-half. Heat to just below the boiling point. Serve hot.

Serves 4

Broccoli Salad

2 bunches broccoli	1/2 cup sugar
1 small onion, chopped	1/4 cup pecans, chopped
1 pound bacon, crisp-cooked and crumbled	1 to 1 1/2 tablespoons apple cider vinegar
1 cup mayonnaise	Lettuce leaves

Cut the broccoli into florets. Combine the onion, bacon, mayonnaise, sugar, pecans and vinegar in a bowl and mix well. Combine with the broccoli in a large bowl just before serving and toss well to coat. Serve immediately on lettuce leaves. Garnish with tomato wedges.

Serves 2 to 4

Red and Green Salad

1 cup mayonnaise	1 pound bacon, crisp-cooked and crumbled
1/2 cup sugar	
1/4 cup vinegar	1/2 cup raisins
1 bunch broccoli, cut into florets	1/2 cup pecans
1 small head red cabbage, shredded	1 small red onion, sliced into rings

Whisk the mayonnaise, sugar and vinegar together in a small bowl. Chill, covered, for 8 to 10 hours. Combine the broccoli, cabbage, bacon, raisins, pecans and onion in a large bowl and toss to mix. Add the dressing just before serving and toss to coat.

Serves 8

Cathy's Really Awesome Crunchy Slaw

1 (3-ounce) package chicken flavor ramen noodles
1/2 cup olive oil
1/3 cup sugar
3 1/4 tablespoons tarragon vinegar
1 head green cabbage, shredded
2 bunches green onions, chopped
3/4 cup toasted sliced almonds
1/4 cup sunflower seeds

Reserve the seasoning packet from the ramen noodles; break the noodles into pieces and set aside.

Combine the olive oil and sugar in a microwave-safe bowl and microwave for 1 minute. Stir in the vinegar and contents of the reserved seasoning packet.

Toss the broken noodles, cabbage, green onions, almonds and sunflower seeds in a large bowl. Stir the dressing and pour over the top of the salad. Toss to coat and serve immediately.

Serves 10

Mandarin Salad

1/4 cup sliced almonds
2 1/2 tablespoons sugar
1 head romaine, torn into pieces
1 head butter lettuce, torn into pieces
1 cup chopped celery
1 bunch green onions, chopped
1 (11-ounce) can mandarin oranges, drained
1/4 cup vegetable oil
2 tablespoons red wine vinegar
2 tablespoons sugar
1 tablespoon chopped parsley
1/2 teaspoon salt

Sauté the almonds with 2 1/2 tablespoons sugar in a small skillet until coated and toasted; do not overbrown. Remove from the heat and let cool; break into pieces.

Toss the lettuces, celery, green onions and oranges in a bowl to mix well.

Whisk the oil, vinegar, 2 tablespoons sugar, parsley and salt together in a small bowl. Pour over the salad and toss to coat. Top with the sugared almonds.

Serves 4

Spinach Salad

5 ounces spinach
2 large Granny Smith apples, chopped
1/2 cup cashew pieces
1/4 cup raisins
Crumbled feta cheese (optional)
1/4 cup olive oil
1/4 cup sugar
2 tablespoons balsamic vinegar
1/4 teaspoon celery salt

Combine the spinach, apples, cashews, raisins and cheese in a large bowl; toss to mix.

Whisk the olive oil, sugar, vinegar and celery salt together in a small bowl. Pour over the salad and toss to coat.

Serves 8 to 10

Strawberry and Spinach Salad

1¹/2 tablespoons sesame seeds

2 ounces slivered almonds

8 ounces spinach leaves, washed and torn into bite-size pieces

1 pint strawberries, sliced

¹/4 cup vegetable oil

¹/4 cup apple cider vinegar

¹/4 cup sugar

1 tablespoon poppy seeds

1¹/2 teaspoons minced onion

¹/4 teaspoon Worcestershire sauce

¹/4 teaspoon paprika

Bake the sesame seeds and almonds on separate baking sheets in a 300-degree oven for 10 minutes or until toasted, watching carefully to prevent overbrowning. Toss the spinach, strawberries and almonds in a large bowl to mix. Whisk the sesame seeds, oil, vinegar, sugar, poppy seeds, onion, Worcestershire sauce and paprika together in a bowl. Pour over the salad and toss to coat.

Serves 4

Best-Ever Grape Salad

1 cup sour cream
8 ounces cream cheese, softened
1/2 to 1 cup granulated sugar
1 teaspoon vanilla extract, or to taste
2 pounds seedless green grapes
2 pounds seedless red grapes
1 cup packed brown sugar
1 cup crushed pecans

Mix the sour cream, cream cheese, granulated sugar and vanilla in a large bowl until blended. Add the grapes and stir until well coated.

Stir the brown sugar and pecans together in a bowl. Sprinkle generously over the grape salad to completely cover.

Chill for 8 to 10 hours before serving.

Serves 6 to 8

Cranberry Salad

Juice of 1 large lemon
1 cup chopped apple
1 (14-ounce) can cranberry sauce
1 (3-ounce) package cherry or
strawberry gelatin

1/2 cup drained crushed pineapple
1/2 cup chopped celery
1 cup chopped nuts
Pinch of salt

Spray a salad mold with nonstick cooking spray or oil lightly. Toss the lemon juice and apple in a bowl to prevent browning. Heat the cranberry sauce and gelatin in the top of a double boiler until melted and combined, stirring occasionally. Stir in the apple, pineapple, celery, nuts and salt. Pour into the prepared mold. Chill in the refrigerator until set.

Serves 6

Lemon-Pineapple Salad

1 (3-ounce) package instant
lemon pudding mix
1 (20-ounce) can crushed pineapple

1 cup miniature marshmallows
1 cup nuts or coconut (optional)
8 ounces whipped topping

Sprinkle the pudding mix over the pineapple in a large bowl and mix well. Stir in the marshmallows and nuts. Fold in the whipped topping. Chill, covered, until serving time.

Serves 6 to 8

Fresh from the Gulf

Ginger Fish

¹/₂ cup soy sauce
¹/₃ cup sake or sherry
1 tablespoon grated fresh ginger
1 tablespoon minced garlic
3 pounds fish, cut into bite-size pieces
²/₃ cup cornstarch
1 teaspoon sugar
Peanut oil for frying

Combine the soy sauce, wine, ginger and garlic in a large bowl and mix well. Add the fish and stir to coat. Marinate in the refrigerator for 2 hours; drain. Mix the cornstarch and sugar together in a shallow bowl. Add the fish pieces to the cornstarch mixture a few at a time and toss until lightly coated. Fry in peanut oil in a large heavy saucepan until the fish flakes easily, working in batches if necessary. Serve hot.

Serves 24

Seafood Safe Handling Tips

*Purchase seafood last, and keep it cold during the trip home.
Keep raw and cooked seafood separate to prevent
bacterial cross-contamination.
After handling raw seafood, thoroughly wash knives,
cutting surfaces, sponges, and hands with hot soapy water.
Marinate seafood in the refrigerator, and discard any used marinade
to avoid bacteria from raw juices. For basting, reserve a portion
of marinade before adding raw seafood.*

La Bella Vista Baked Flounder

2 flounder fillets	Lemon wedges
Salt and pepper to taste	Melted butter
1 onion, thinly sliced	Crushed butter crackers
1 bell pepper, thinly sliced	

Remove the skin from the flounder. Cut each fillet into four smaller fillets and season both sides with salt and pepper. Arrange in a shallow baking dish. Lay the onion and bell pepper evenly over the fish to just cover, reserving any unused portion for another purpose. Squeeze lemon juice over the top and drizzle with butter. Sprinkle with cracker crumbs to lightly cover the top. Bake in the bottom of a broiler for 3 to 4 minutes or until the fish flakes easily. Serve with jasmine rice and steamed fresh broccoli.

Note: This recipe can be doubled easily. Increase the cooking time as needed. Thicker fillets should be butterflied to keep them from drying out.

Serves 1 or 2

Fish Buying and Storing Tips

Meat should be firm, with a fresh sea breeze aroma and no discoloration. Store fresh fish in the coldest part of the refrigerator (32° F.) for up to 2 days. To freeze, wrap fish tightly to prevent freezer burn. Date the package and store at 0° F. for up to 2 months. Thaw in the refrigerator or under cold running water.

Bill's Island-Style Fish Casserole

2¹/2 to 3 pounds grouper fillets
1 cup olive oil
1 envelope dry onion soup mix
1 (10-ounce) can Cheddar cheese soup
1 (10-ounce) can cream of mushroom soup
¹/2 cup milk
1 (6-ounce) can tuna, drained
1 pound shrimp, peeled and deveined
2 tablespoons lemon herb seasoning
1 cup all-purpose flour
¹/4 cup bread crumbs

Cut the grouper into 2- to 3-inch pieces and combine with the olive oil in a bowl. Marinate, covered, for 30 to 60 minutes; drain.

Combine the soup mix, cheese soup, mushroom soup, milk and tuna in a saucepan and mix well. Cook over low heat until heated through, stirring constantly. Add the shrimp and cook for 5 minutes longer.

Spoon enough of the shrimp sauce to lightly cover the bottom into a 9×13-inch baking dish. Sprinkle the grouper with the lemon herb seasoning and coat with the flour. Arrange in the prepared baking dish. Pour the remaining shrimp sauce over the top. Sprinkle with the bread crumbs. Bake at 325 degrees for 30 minutes.

Note: You may substitute amberjack or snapper for the grouper.

Serves 6

Grilled Grouper

1/2 cup pitted kalamata olives
1/4 cup plain bread crumbs
1 tablespoon capers
1 teaspoon lemon juice
1 garlic clove
1 teaspoon olive oil
4 (4-ounce) grouper fillets

Place a grill pan on a grill over high heat. Combine the olives, bread crumbs, capers, lemon juice, garlic and olive oil in a food processor and process until smooth. Brush both sides of the grouper with some of the olive mixture and arrange in the prepared grill pan. Grill, uncovered, for 5 minutes. Brush with additional olive mixture. Turn the grouper and grill for an additional 5 minutes or until the fish flakes easily. Serve with lime wedges.

Serves 4

Caper Sauce

1 cup mayonnaise
3 tablespoons drained capers

Combine the mayonnaise and capers in a bowl; mix well. Serve with fish.

Makes 1 cup

Bacon and Olive Fish with Creamy Corn Relish

Creamy Corn Relish
1 (15-ounce) can low-sodium whole kernel corn, drained
1 cup chopped mixed fresh tomato, onion and bell pepper
1/4 cup sliced green onions
1/4 teaspoon pepper
1/4 cup ranch salad dressing

Bacon and Olive Fish
1 pint cherry tomatoes, cut into quarters
I (4-ounce) jar garlic-stuffed olives, drained and chopped
1 cup chopped red onion
2 tablespoons olive oil
4 slices thick-cut bacon, cut into halves
4 grouper fillets (about 1 1/2 pounds)
1/8 teaspoon ground pepper

For the relish, combine the corn, tomato mix, green onions and pepper in a bowl. Stir in the salad dressing. Chill, covered, until serving time. Stir once before serving.

For the fish, combine the tomatoes, olives, onion and olive oil in a bowl. Arrange the bacon in a single layer in a preheated large sauté pan over medium heat. Cook for 1 to 2 minutes or until the bacon begins to crisp. Season the fish with the pepper and arrange over the bacon in the pan. Reduce the heat to medium-low. Cook, covered, for 4 to 5 minutes without turning. Spoon the olive mixture over the grouper. Cook, covered, for 3 to 4 minutes or until the grouper registers 145 degrees on a meat thermometer or until it flakes easily. Serve with Creamy Corn Relish.

Serves 4

Tomato-Poached Grouper with Sautéed Vegetables

8 ounces sliced mushrooms
3 baby zucchini or summer squash, sliced
1 (14-ounce) can diced tomatoes with
green peppers and onions
1/2 teaspoon dried oregano
1 teaspoon thinly sliced fresh basil
1 pound grouper fillets
Salt and pepper to taste

Sauté the mushrooms and zucchini in a well-oiled large skillet over medium heat for 2 to 3 minutes, stirring occasionally. Add the tomatoes, oregano and basil and simmer for 2 to 3 minutes. Push the vegetables to one side of the skillet. Add the fish to the skillet and spoon the vegetables over the top. Simmer, tightly covered, for 6 minutes or until the fish flakes easily. Season with salt and pepper before serving.

Serves 4

Cooking Tips

*Cook fish at 400° F. for 10 minutes per inch of thickness
of the fillet or steak.
Cook until the meat is opaque and flakes easily with a fork.
Cook thoroughly but do not overcook.
To grill, use a grill basket to prevent the meat
from falling through the grill.*

Pecan Parmesan Grouper

1 tablespoon butter
1 tablespoon vegetable oil
2 tablespoons all-purpose flour
3/4 cup (3 ounces) grated Parmesan cheese
6 (4-ounce) grouper fillets or other firm white fish
1 egg, beaten
1/2 cup chopped pecans

Melt the butter in a shallow baking pan in a 425-degree oven. Remove from the oven and add the oil, swirling to coat the pan. Maintain the oven temperature. Combine the flour and cheese in a shallow dish. Dip the grouper into the egg, then roll in the flour mixture to coat. Arrange in the prepared pan. Sprinkle with the pecans. Bake for 10 to 15 minutes or until the fish flakes easily.

Serves 6

How Much to Buy

Fillets or steaks — 1/4 to 1/3 pound per serving
Whole or drawn fish — 3/4 to 1 pound per serving
Dressed whole fish — 1/2 pound per serving

Pecan-Crusted Grouper

1/2 cup pecans, finely chopped
1/2 cup bread crumbs
4 (4-ounce) grouper fillets
Salt and pepper to taste
1/3 cup all-purpose flour
2 eggs, beaten
3/4 cup (11/2 sticks) butter or margarine
Juice of 1 lemon
1 bunch parsley, chopped

Process the pecans and bread crumbs in a food processor until finely ground. Spoon into a shallow dish. Season the grouper with salt and pepper. Dredge in the flour, then dip into the eggs. Coat with the pecan mixture.

Melt 1/4 cup of the butter in a nonstick ovenproof skillet over medium-high heat. Add the grouper and cook until light brown, then turn. Bake at 400 degrees for 10 minutes or until the fish flakes easily.

Remove the fish to a serving platter, reserving the cooking liquid in the skillet. Add the remaining 1/2 cup butter to the skillet. Cook over high heat until the butter foams and turns light brown, stirring constantly. Stir in the lemon juice and parsley. Pour over the grouper and serve immediately.

Serves 4

Baked Redfish in Rosemary Tomato Sauce

1 (3- to 4-pound) whole redfish
Salt and pepper to taste
2 small yellow onions, sliced into rounds
1/4 cup (1/2 stick) butter, chilled and cut into pieces
4 sprigs of rosemary
1/2 cup pinot grigio
1 (28-ounce) can crushed tomatoes

Line a large baking dish with heavy-duty foil and spray with nonstick cooking spray. Clean and scale the redfish and place in the prepared baking dish. Sprinkle salt and pepper on both sides and inside the cavity. Cut slits to the bone every 2 inches from the head to tail. Insert onion slices and butter pieces into each slit. Place any unused portions in the cavity. Arrange the rosemary in the cavity. Pour the wine over the redfish. Spread the tomatoes evenly over the top.

Bake at 375 degrees for 45 to 60 minutes or until the fish flakes easily, basting with the pan juices occasionally.

Serves 4 to 6

Baked Salmon

3 to 4 tablespoons soy sauce
3 to 4 tablespoons zesty Italian
salad dressing
4 garlic cloves, minced
1 tablespoon grated fresh ginger
1 tablespoon (heaping) brown sugar
1 whole fillet of salmon or sea trout
1 tablespoon dry mustard
(Coleman's preferred)
1 tablespoon water
1/4 cup mayonnaise, or to taste

Mix the soy sauce and salad dressing in a small bowl. Pour into a 9×13-inch baking pan, tilting to cover the bottom of the pan. Add the garlic, ginger and brown sugar and stir to mix. Add the salmon and marinate for 30 to 45 minutes. Bake at 400 degrees for 20 minutes or until the fish flakes easily.

Stir the dry mustard and water together in a bowl. Add the mayonnaise and mix well. Serve the mustard sauce with the salmon.

Note: The mustard sauce is also excellent with other fish and with shrimp.

Serves 8 to 10

Ginger Soy Baked Salmon

1 teaspoon lemon juice
1/4 teaspoon soy sauce
1/2 teaspoon ground ginger
1/4 teaspoon cinnamon
1/8 teaspoon pepper
1 (12-ounce) fresh salmon fillet

Whisk the lemon juice, soy sauce, ginger, cinnamon and pepper together in a small bowl. Place the salmon in a baking pan and pour the lemon juice mixture over the top. Bake at 325 degrees for 25 minutes or until the fish flakes easily.

Serves 4

The Quilting Group

*Every Tuesday morning, ladies from the Island gather at the
Civic Club to quilt. They are not quilting just any quilt, but
THE Seafood Festival Quilt. The stunning work of art is raffled off each year
on the first weekend in November at the Florida Seafood Festival
held in Apalachicola. Proceeds from the raffle benefit the St. George Island
Volunteer Fire Department and First Responder Unit, and the raffle
has raised thousands of dollars. The one-of-a-kind quilts, lovingly stitched
by the quilting group, are designed by a local artist and depict
something concerning the Island. Each year everyone says the quilts
can't get any better, but somehow they do!*

Cape Cod Crab Cakes

1 egg, beaten
1/4 cup finely chopped red bell pepper
1/4 cup finely chopped green onions
2 tablespoons chopped cilantro
2 tablespoon low-fat mayonnaise
2 teaspoons Dijon mustard
1 1/2 teaspoons crab boil seasoning
1/2 teaspoon hot red pepper sauce
1/2 teaspoon Worcestershire sauce
1/4 teaspoon curry powder
1/4 teaspoon each, salt and pepper
1 pound fresh lump crab meat, shells removed
1 1/3 cups panko (Japanese bread crumbs)
2 tablespoons vegetable oil

Combine the egg, bell pepper, green onions, cilantro, mayonnaise, Dijon mustard, crab boil seasoning, hot sauce, Worcestershire sauce, curry powder, salt and pepper in a bowl and mix well. Fold in the crab meat and bread crumbs, taking care not to break up the large pieces of crab meat. The mixture will be loose. Shape 1/3 cupfuls into 3-inch patties. Heat the oil in an electric skillet. Fry the crab cakes in the oil until light brown. Serve immediately.

Serves 8

Jerry's Crab Cakes

Jerry's Seafood Tartar Sauce

1 cup mayonnaise	1 tablespoon capers, drained
1/3 cup finely chopped dill pickles	1 teaspoon Worcestershire sauce
1/3 cup finely chopped green onions	1/4 teaspoon garlic powder
1/2 small jalapeño chile, seeded and chopped	1/4 teaspoon hot sauce
	Dash of artificial sweetener

Crab Cakes

2 or 3 green onions, finely chopped	1/4 teaspoon garlic powder
1/2 cup finely chopped red bell pepper	Dash of cayenne pepper
1 egg, beaten	Salt and black pepper to taste
1/4 cup mayonnaise	1/2 cup bread crumbs or crushed saltine crackers
2 teaspoons Worcestershire sauce	
Juice of 1/2 large lemon	1 pound crab meat, shells removed
1/4 teaspoon hot sauce	All-purpose flour for dusting
1 teaspoon dry mustard	1/2 cup peanut oil or vegetable oil

For the tartar sauce, combine the mayonnaise, pickles, green onions, jalapeño, capers, Worcestershire sauce, garlic powder, hot sauce and sweetener in a bowl and mix well. Chill, covered, until serving time.

For the crab cakes, combine the green onions, bell pepper, egg, mayonnaise, Worcestershire sauce, lemon juice, hot sauce, dry mustard, garlic powder, cayenne pepper, salt and black pepper in a large bowl and mix well. Fold in the bread crumbs and crab meat, taking care not to break up the large pieces of crab meat. Shape into 4 to 6 patties and dust both sides with flour. Heat the peanut oil in a skillet over medium heat. Fry the patties in the oil for 4 minutes or until golden brown. Turn and fry until golden brown on both sides. Serve with the Tartar Sauce.

Serves 4 to 6

Sylvia's Crab Cakes

Crab Cake Sauce

3/4 cup mayonnaise
2 tablespoons Dijon mustard
2 tablespoons honey
1 tablespoon red wine vinegar

1 tablespoon chopped fresh parsley
1/2 teaspoon Old Bay seasoning
1/2 teaspoon chili powder
1/4 teaspoon pepper

Crab Cakes

1 egg, beaten
2 tablespoons mayonnaise
1 tablespoon spicy brown mustard
1 teaspoon Worcestershire sauce
1 tablespoon finely chopped parsley
1/4 teaspoon salt

1 pound lump crab meat, shells
 removed
1 cup (about) Italian bread crumbs
2 tablespoons butter
1 tablespoon vegetable oil

For the sauce, whisk the mayonnaise, Dijon mustard, honey and vinegar together in a bowl. Stir in the parsley, Old Bay seasoning, chili powder and pepper. Chill, covered, until serving time.

For the crab cakes, mix the egg, mayonnaise, mustard, Worcestershire sauce, parsley and salt in a bowl. Fold in the crab meat, taking care not to break up the large pieces. Shape into 3-inch patties and coat lightly with the bread crumbs. Chill the patties for 1 hour.

Melt the butter with the oil in a skillet. Add the patties and fry until light brown and heated through. Serve hot with the Crab Cake Sauce.

Serves 6 to 8

Oysters à la St. George

4 ounces saltine crackers, crushed
1 pint (or more) shucked oysters
1 (16-ounce) can cream-style corn
1¹/2 teaspoons salt
1¹/2 teaspoons pepper
¹/2 cup (1 stick) margarine,
cut into pieces
3 eggs, beaten
2 to 3 cups evaporated milk

Alternate layers of cracker crumbs, oysters, corn, salt, pepper and margarine in a greased baking dish, beginning and ending with cracker crumbs. Beat the eggs with the evaporated milk in a small bowl. Pour over the layers. Bake at 450 degrees for 30 minutes.

Notes: You may use egg substitute and evaporated skim milk in this recipe, if desired. Oysters à la St. George was a prizewinner in 1967.

Serves 8

The Mighty Oyster

Ninety percent of Florida's oyster crop is grown in Apalachicola Bay, one of the most ideal environments for the growth and culture of oysters. The Apalachicola Bay oyster is medium-sized, with a round, pointed green shell and a large cup. The oyster is firm with a mild, slightly sweet flavor. . . the best in the world!

Island Time Scallops

16 ounces orzo
1¹/2 pounds scallops
2 garlic cloves, chopped
Vegetable oil for sautéing
¹/2 cup chopped fresh basil
¹/4 cup chopped fresh parsley
1 (14-ounce) can chopped tomatoes
1 pound sliced mushrooms
1 teaspoon salt
1 teaspoon pepper
³/4 cup chopped green onions
1 cup crumbled feta cheese

Cook the pasta according to the package directions; drain. Sauté the scallops and garlic in a small amount of oil in a large skillet for several minutes. Add the basil and parsley and cook for several minutes longer. Remove the scallops, garlic, basil and parsley to a large bowl using a slotted spoon, reserving the drippings in the skillet.

Add the tomatoes, mushrooms, salt and pepper to the skillet and cook for several minutes. Add the green onions and cook until the mushrooms and green onions are softened. Add to the scallop mixture and mix well. Stir in the orzo and cheese. Top with additional cheese.

Serves 6

Scallops with Pasta and Pine Nuts

8 ounces fettuccini
1/4 cup olive oil, plus more for drizzling
3 garlic cloves, minced
1 leek, thinly sliced (white portion only)
10 pitted large black olives, cut into halves
1/4 cup pine nuts
12 large sea scallops
Salt and pepper to taste
2 tablespoons chopped fresh basil
1 cup (4 ounces) grated Parmesan cheese

Cook the pasta according to the package directions; drain and return to the pan. Drizzle with olive oil to prevent sticking. Heat 1/4 cup olive oil in a skillet. Add the garlic and leek and cook until softened but not brown. Add the olives and pine nuts and sauté until the pine nuts are very light brown. Add the scallops and cook until opaque and slightly firm. Season with salt and pepper. Add to the pasta with the basil and toss to mix well. Sprinkle with the cheese and serve.

Serves 4

Scallops Primavera

1 small onion, sliced

3 garlic cloves, minced

1 tablespoon dried oregano

Pinch of hot pepper flakes, or to taste

2 tablespoons olive oil

16 ounces Roma tomatoes, seeded and chopped

1 large red bell pepper, cut into bite-size pieces

1 large yellow bell pepper, cut into bite-size pieces

1 large orange bell pepper, cut into bite-size pieces

2 small zucchini, chopped

1 cup chicken stock

1 pound scallops

2 tablespoons olive oil

Hot cooked pasta

Grated Parmesan cheese

Sauté the onion, garlic, oregano and pepper flakes in 2 tablespoons olive oil in a large sauté pan for 1 minute. Add the tomatoes, bell peppers and zucchini and sauté for 2 to 3 minutes longer. Add the stock and cook for 2 to 3 minutes.

Sauté the scallops in 2 tablespoons olive oil in a large nonstick skillet for 3 minutes. Add to the vegetable mixture and bring to a boil. Boil until the scallops are opaque and slightly firm. Spoon over hot cooked pasta to serve. Sprinkle with Parmesan cheese.

Serves 6

Barbecue Shrimp

1 pound unpeeled shrimp
Olive oil
Cracked pepper to taste
Salt to taste
Lemon juice to taste
Hot sauce to taste
Worcestershire sauce to taste
Butter, cut into pieces

Arrange the shrimp in a single layer in a large shallow baking dish. Drizzle with olive oil. Season very liberally with pepper. Sprinkle heavily with salt, lemon juice, hot sauce and Worcestershire sauce, keeping in mind that the seasoning needs to penetrate the shells of the shrimp. Top with butter. Broil for 15 to 20 minutes or until the shrimp turn pink. Spread on newspapers to serve. Have plenty of napkins available.

Note: The shrimp are best served with French bread, cold beer, and a green salad.

Serves 3 or 4

Grilled Shrimp

1/4 cup (1/2 stick) butter, melted
2 garlic cloves, minced
1 1/2 tablespoons vegetable oil
1 tablespoon minced garlic
1 teaspoon thyme
1 teaspoon oregano
1 teaspoon paprika
1/2 teaspoon salt
Pinch of cayenne pepper
2 pounds shrimp, peeled and deveined

Combine the butter and 2 garlic cloves in a small bowl and mix well; keep warm. Whisk the oil, 1 tablespoon minced garlic, thyme, oregano, paprika, salt and cayenne pepper together in a large bowl. Add the shrimp and toss to coat. Marinate, covered, in the refrigerator for 1 to 6 hours. Thread the shrimp onto skewers. Grill over medium heat for 4 to 6 minutes or until the shrimp turn pink, turning once halfway through the cooking process. Remove to a serving platter and drizzle with the warm garlic butter.

Serves 4

Cajun Shrimp Casserole

1/4 cup (1/2 stick) butter
1 small red onion, chopped
1/2 cup chopped red bell pepper
1/2 cup chopped yellow bell pepper
1/2 cup chopped green bell pepper
4 garlic cloves, minced
2 cups frozen sliced okra
1 tablespoon lemon juice
11/2 teaspoons salt
2 pounds large shrimp, peeled and deveined
1 (10-ounce) can cream of shrimp soup
1/2 cup dry white wine
1 tablespoon soy sauce
1/4 teaspoon cayenne pepper
3 cups cooked long grain rice
1/4 cup (1 ounce) grated Parmesan cheese

Melt the butter in a large skillet over medium-high heat. Add the onion and bell peppers. Sauté for 7 minutes or until tender. Add the garlic and sauté for 1 minute. Stir in the okra, lemon juice and salt and cook for 5 minutes. Add the shrimp and cook for 3 minutes or until the shrimp turn pink. Stir in the soup, wine, soy sauce, cayenne pepper and rice.

Spoon into a lightly greased 7×11-inch baking dish. Sprinkle with the cheese. Bake at 350 degrees for 15 to 20 minutes or until bubbly and light brown. Garnish with parsley sprigs.

Serves 6

Chicken and Shrimp Loaf

3 large chicken breasts
Salt and pepper to taste
1 pound jumbo shrimp, peeled and deveined
8 ounces French bread, torn into pieces
2 cups milk
1 green bell pepper, roasted, seeded and chopped
2 eggs
8 ounces crushed pineapple, drained
8 ounces goat cheese, crumbled
1 teaspoon Old Bay seasoning
1/2 teaspoon thyme

Season the chicken with salt and pepper and arrange in a baking dish. Bake at 350 degrees for 50 minutes. Let cool slightly, then cut into bite-size pieces. Maintain the oven temperature.

Season the shrimp with salt and pepper and arrange on a baking sheet. Bake for 10 minutes. Let cool slightly, then chop. Maintain the oven temperature.

Soak the bread in the milk in a large bowl for 30 minutes.

Add the chicken, shrimp, bell pepper, eggs, pineapple, cheese, Old Bay seasoning and thyme to the bread mixture and mix well. Spoon into a food processor. Process to a fine purée. Spoon into an ovenproof plastic bag. Seal the bag and place in a loaf pan. Bake, covered with foil, for 1 hour. Let cool completely.

Chill for 8 to 10 hours. Remove from the plastic bag. Serve with salad greens, crackers or bread.

Serves 6 to 8

Garlic Shrimp with Herbed Butter and Lemon Rice

Herbed Dipping Butter
1 cup (2 sticks) salted butter, melted
2 to 3 teaspoons minced fresh herbs,
such as Italian parsley, basil, oregano, thyme and/or bronze fennel
2 teaspoons fresh lemon or lime juice
Freshly ground pepper to taste

Lemon and Parsley Rice
1 cup basmati rice
1/3 cup minced parsley
Juice of 1 large lemon
4 small green onions, thinly sliced (optional)

For the dipping butter, combine the butter, herbs, lemon juice and pepper in a small saucepan and mix well. Heat through; keep warm until serving time.

For the rice, cook the rice according to the package directions; keep warm. Just before serving time, toss with the parsley and lemon juice in a large bowl. Top with the green onions.

Garlic Shrimp

3/4 cup extra-virgin olive oil
2 to 3 pounds jumbo fresh shrimp, peeled and deveined, tails intact
2 large garlic cloves, minced
1 cup (scant) chopped fresh green herbs, such as Italian parsley,
basil, oregano, thyme and/or bronze fennel
Juice of 2 small lemons or 1 large lemon
2 teaspoons kosher salt

For the shrimp, heat the olive oil in a large skillet. Add the shrimp and garlic and cook until the shrimp turn pink. Add the herbs, lemon juice and salt and mix well. Serve with the Lemon and Parsley Rice and small bowls of the Herbed Dipping Butter. Garnish with lemon wedges.

Serves 4

Shrimp and Creamy Grits

Creamy Grits

6 cups chicken broth
1 cup heavy cream
2 cups stone-ground grits

2 tablespoons butter
1/2 teaspoon salt

Shrimp

6 slices bacon
1 red bell pepper, thinly sliced
1 green bell pepper, thinly sliced
1 onion, thinly sliced
2 pounds peeled deveined shrimp

1/2 teaspoon Cajun seasoning
1/2 cup dry sherry
1 teaspoon cornstarch and
    water slurry
1 bunch green onions, chopped

For the grits, bring the broth and cream to a boil in a 3-quart saucepan. Whisk in the grits gradually. Reduce the heat. Simmer, covered, for 30 minutes, stirring occasionally. Stir in the butter and salt; keep warm.

For the shrimp, cook the bacon in a large skillet until crisp; remove with a slotted spoon, reserving the drippings in the skillet. Let the bacon cool slightly, then chop.

Add the bell pepper and onion to the pan drippings and sauté for 2 minutes. Add the shrimp and Cajun seasoning. Cook until the shrimp begin to turn pink. Stir in the sherry and slurry. Cook, covered, for 5 minutes over medium heat.

Spread the Creamy Grits in a 9×13-inch serving dish. Top with the shrimp mixture. Sprinkle with the bacon and green onions and serve.

Serves 6 to 8

Shrimp and Grits

4 cups stone-ground grits
1/2 cup chopped pancetta
2 tablespoons olive oil
2 tablespoons chopped green onions
2 tablespoons chopped onion
2 tablespoons chopped green bell pepper
20 large shrimp, peeled, tails intact
2 tablespoons white wine
1 cup heavy cream
1/4 teaspoon salt
1/4 teaspoon pepper

Prepare the grits according to the package directions; keep warm. Sauté the pancetta in the olive oil in a large sauté pan over medium-high heat until crisp. Add the green onions, onion and bell pepper and sauté until tender, stirring frequently.

Remove from the heat and add the shrimp. Allow to cook in the hot pan for 2 minutes. Return the pan to the heat and stir in the wine, cream, salt and pepper. Divide the grits among serving bowls and top evenly with the shrimp mixture.

Serves 4

Creole Shrimp

4 pounds unpeeled shrimp
1/2 cup (1 stick) butter
1/2 cup olive oil
1/3 cup chili sauce
1/4 cup Worcestershire sauce
4 garlic cloves, minced
2 tablespoons Creole seasoning
2 tablespoons lemon juice
1 teaspoon oregano
1 teaspoon paprika
1 teaspoon ground red pepper
1 teaspoon hot sauce

Spread the shrimp in a shallow foil-lined broiler pan. Combine the butter, olive oil, chili sauce, Worcestershire sauce, garlic, Creole seasoning, lemon juice, oregano, paprika, red pepper and hot sauce in a saucepan. Heat until the butter melts, stirring frequently. Pour evenly over the shrimp and stir to mix well. Chill, covered, for 1 hour, turning after 30 minutes.

Bake, uncovered, at 400 degrees for 20 minutes or until the shrimp turn pink, turning after 10 minutes. Serve hot with bread.

Serves 8

Low-Country Shrimp Boil

8 to 10 red potatoes
1/4 cup salt
2 packets Old Bay seasoning
6 lemons, cut into halves
10 to 12 ears of corn, cut into halves
4 onions, cut into quarters
2 pounds andouille or kielbasa
5 pounds shrimp, deveined

Fill a 3-gallon or larger stockpot halfway with water. Add the potatoes, salt and Old Bay seasoning and bring to a boil. Squeeze the lemon juice into the water, then add the lemons. Boil for 10 minutes longer. Add the corn, onions and sausage and boil for 10 minutes. Add the shrimp and boil for 1 minute or until the shrimp turn pink; drain. Spoon into a shallow bowl. Place newspapers on the table and have plenty of paper towels available—easy cleanup! Serve with drawn butter and cocktail sauce.

Note: A low-country boil is an easy, fun meal to share with family or friends.

Serves 10

Piña Colada Shrimp

Canola oil for frying
3/4 cup coconut milk
6 tablespoons pineapple preserves
3 tablespoons cornstarch
1 teaspoon Worcestershire sauce
1 cup shredded unsweetened coconut
1 cup panko (Japanese bread crumbs)
1 pound shrimp, peeled and deveined, tails intact
1/4 cup cornstarch

Heat 1 inch of canola oil to 360 degrees in a large sauté pan over medium-high heat. Whisk the coconut milk, preserves, 3 tablespoons cornstarch and Worcestershire sauce together in a bowl. Combine the coconut and bread crumbs in a shallow dish.

Toss the shrimp with 1/4 cup cornstarch, shaking off any excess. Dip in the coconut milk mixture, then coat in the bread crumb mixture. Carefully drop the shrimp one at a time into the hot oil. Fry in batches for 3 minutes or until golden brown. Remove the shrimp to a paper towel-lined plate to drain before serving.

Serves 8

Shrimp Étouffée

1 onion, chopped
1/4 cup chopped celery
1/2 cup (1 stick) butter, cut into pieces
3 pounds shrimp, peeled and deveined
2 (10-ounce) cans cream of shrimp soup
1/4 cup Key West lime juice
1 teaspoon Creole seasoning
1/2 teaspoon gumbo filé
1 large bay leaf
1 teaspoon thyme leaves, crushed
1 garlic clove, chopped
1/4 cup all-purpose flour
3 cups yellow rice, cooked

Sauté the onion and celery in the butter in a large skillet until softened. Add the shrimp and cook until pink. Stir in the soup, lime juice, Creole seasoning, gumbo filé, bay leaf, thyme and garlic. Sprinkle the flour over everything and stir to mix well. Simmer, tightly covered, for 10 minutes, stirring occasionally. Serve over the rice.

Serves 8

J. B.'s Scampi

1/2 cup (1 stick) unsalted light butter
1/4 cup extra-virgin olive oil
1/2 cup white wine
6 garlic cloves, minced
1/3 envelope Italian salad dressing mix,
or 1/4 cup Italian salad dressing
Juice of 1/2 lemon
1/2 teaspoon coarse sea salt
1/4 teaspoon cayenne pepper
40 extra-large fresh Gulf shrimp,
head-on

1 cup cold water
16 ounces spaghetti or pasta of choice
1/4 cup small capers
1/2 cup coarsely chopped kalamata
olives
1 tablespoon chopped fresh Italian
parsley
Grated zest of 1/2 lemon
1 teaspoon extra-virgin olive oil
Freshly cracked black pepper to taste

Melt the butter with 1/4 cup olive oil in a very large skillet. Add the wine, garlic, salad dressing mix, lemon juice, salt and cayenne pepper and mix well. Cook over medium heat until the wine is reduced, stirring constantly.

Remove the heads from the shrimp and reserve. Peel the shrimp, discarding the shells. Combine the reserved shrimp heads with the water in a small saucepan and bring to a boil. Boil until reduced to 1/2 cup; strain, discarding the shrimp heads.

Cook the pasta to al dente according to the package directions; drain, reserving some of the cooking liquid. Add the shrimp and reduced shrimp stock to the wine mixture and cook over medium heat for 3 to 4 minutes or just until the shrimp turn pink.

Reduce the heat to low. Add the pasta and mix well. Fold in the capers and olives. Spoon the pasta mixture onto a large serving platter. Sprinkle with the parsley and lemon zest. Drizzle with 1 teaspoon olive oil and season with black pepper; do not stir. Serve with spinach salad and warm French bread.

Note: Add finely chopped fresh garden tomatoes when in season. Keep cold until ready to add. Fold in with the capers and olives or sprinkle over the top.

Serves 4 to 6

94

Grilled Marinated Shrimp

1/4 cup olive oil
2 tablespoons lemon juice
1 tablespoon chopped parsley
2 teaspoons freshly ground pepper
3/4 teaspoon dried basil
1/2 teaspoon dried oregano

1/4 teaspoon garlic salt, or
   2 garlic cloves, minced
1/4 teaspoon salt
1 pound shrimp, peeled
   and deveined

Whisk the olive oil, lemon juice, parsley, pepper, basil, oregano, garlic salt and salt together in a bowl. Pour over the shrimp in a bowl or sealable plastic bag. Marinate in the refrigerator for 1 hour or longer; drain. Thread 5 or 6 shrimp onto each skewer. Grill over hot coals for 3 minutes or until the shrimp turn pink.

Serves a variable amount

Easy Creole Tartar Sauce

1/2 cup mayonnaise
2 teaspoons sweet pickle relish
1 teaspoon Creole mustard

Dash of lemon juice
Dash of Creole seasoning
Dash of hot sauce, or to taste

Combine the mayonnaise, pickle relish, mustard, lemon juice, Creole seasoning and hot sauce in a bowl and mix well. Taste and adjust the seasonings. Chill until serving time.

Makes about 1/2 cup

Simply Shrimp

3 tablespoons unsalted butter
3 tablespoons olive oil
1 large onion, chopped
2 garlic cloves, minced
3 pounds Gulf shrimp, peeled
and deveined
3/4 cup chicken broth
3/4 cup Italian salad dressing
1/2 cup white wine

1/2 teaspoon basil
1/2 teaspoon oregano
1/2 teaspoon salt
1/4 teaspoon black pepper
1/8 teaspoon cayenne pepper
1/4 cup chopped parsley
2 to 3 cups rice or fettuccini,
cooked and drained

Melt the butter with the olive oil in a large skillet. Add the onion and garlic and sauté until softened. Stir in the shrimp, broth, salad dressing, wine, basil, oregano, salt, black pepper and cayenne pepper. Bring to a boil; boil until the shrimp turn pink. Remove from the heat. Stir in the parsley, then let stand for 5 minutes. Serve over the hot cooked rice.

Serves 6 to 8

Danny's Seafood Linguini

1/2 cup chopped onion
3 garlic cloves, minced
3 tablespoons olive oil
1 tablespoon all-purpose flour
1/2 teaspoon coriander (do not omit)
3 tablespoons dry white wine
1 cup heavy cream
8 ounces shrimp, peeled
8 ounces bay scallops
12 ounces linguini, cooked and drained

Sauté the onion and garlic in the olive oil in a skillet until softened. Stir in the flour and coriander and cook for 1 minute. Stir in the wine and cream. Bring to a boil, stirring frequently. Add the shrimp and scallops. Reduce the heat and simmer for 5 minutes. Serve over the pasta. Garnish with chopped fresh parsley.

Serves 6 to 8

From the Mainland

Beef Burgundy

2 slices bacon
1 bunch green onions, sliced
2 pounds lean beef, cut into 1-inch pieces
2 cups burgundy
1 1/2 cups beef bouillon
1/4 teaspoon thyme
Salt to taste
3 tablespoons cornstarch
8 ounces sliced mushrooms (optional)
Butter

Cook the bacon in a Dutch oven until crisp. Remove the bacon to a plate, reserving the drippings in the pan. Crumble the bacon. Add the green onions to the reserved drippings and cook until light brown. Add the beef and cook until brown on all sides. Add the wine, bouillon, thyme and salt. Cook, covered, over low heat for 2 hours.

Mix the cornstarch with a small amount of water in a cup. Add to the beef mixture and cook until thickened. Sauté the mushrooms in butter in a sauté pan until softened. Spoon the beef and gravy into a serving bowl. Top with the mushrooms and bacon. Serve hot.

Serves 8

Five-Hour Beef Stew

2 to 3 pounds beef stew meat
1 pound carrots, peeled and sliced
1 bunch celery, chopped
1 large onion, chopped
2 pounds potatoes, peeled and chopped
1/4 cup sugar
1/4 cup cornstarch
2 (14-ounce) cans beef stock
1 (28-ounce) can crushed tomatoes
1 (10-ounce) package frozen peas

Combine the beef, carrots, celery, onion and potatoes in a 5-quart Dutch oven. Whisk the sugar and cornstarch into the stock in a bowl. Pour over the beef and vegetables. Stir in the tomatoes. Bake at 250 degrees for 5 hours. Remove from the oven and stir in the peas until warmed through. Serve hot.

Serves 8

Slow-Cooker Beef with Red Wine Sauce

3 pounds beef stew meat
1 onion, sliced
1 pound fresh mushrooms, cut into halves
1 envelope brown gravy mix
1 cup red wine
2 tablespoons tomato paste
1 (14-ounce) can beef broth
1 bay leaf

Combine the beef, onion and mushrooms in a slow cooker. Whisk the gravy mix, wine, tomato paste and broth together in a bowl. Pour over the beef and vegetables. Add the bay leaf. Cook on High for 6 hours. Discard the bay leaf before serving.

Serves 6

Beef and Wild Rice Casserole

1 (6-ounce) package wild rice mix
1 pound ground beef
1 (10-ounce) can cream of mushroom soup
1 cup mayonnaise
1 cup beef broth or beef bouillon
1 (8-ounce) can sliced water chestnuts
2 (15-ounce) cans cut or French-style green beans, drained
1 cup (4 ounces) shredded Cheddar cheese

Prepare the wild rice according to the package directions. Brown the beef in a large skillet, stirring until crumbly; drain. Combine the rice, beef, soup, mayonnaise, broth, water chestnuts, green beans and 1/2 cup of the cheese in a bowl and mix well.

Spoon into a 9×13-inch or 2-quart baking dish. Bake at 350 degrees for 45 minutes. Top with the remaining 1/2 cup cheese and bake for 15 minutes longer.

Note: You may substitute 3 cups chopped cooked chicken or turkey for the beef and cream of chicken or cream of celery soup for the mushroom soup. If using chicken or turkey, substitute chicken broth for the beef broth. This casserole freezes well.

Serves 8 to 10

Sour Cream Noodle Bake

1¹⁄4 pounds ground chuck
1 (15-ounce) can tomato sauce
¹⁄2 teaspoon salt
Freshly ground pepper to taste
8 ounces egg noodles
¹⁄2 cup sour cream
1¹⁄4 cups small curd cottage cheese
¹⁄2 cup sliced green onions
1 cup (4 ounces) shredded Cheddar cheese

Brown the beef in a large skillet, stirring until crumbly; drain. Stir in the tomato sauce, salt and pepper. Simmer over low heat while preparing the remaining ingredients.

Cook the egg noodles to al dente according to the package directions; drain. Combine the sour cream and cottage cheese in a bowl and mix well. Season generously with pepper. Add the cooked noodles and stir to coat well. Stir in the green onions.

Spread half the noodle mixture in a 9×9-inch baking dish. Top with half the beef mixture, then sprinkle with half the Cheddar cheese. Repeat the layers. Bake at 350 degrees for 20 minutes or until the cheese melts.

Serves 8

Kick-Butt Ribs

3 racks of ribs
Salt to taste
$1/2$ cup paprika
1 tablespoon fine black pepper
1 tablespoon sea salt
1 tablespoon chili powder
1 tablespoon onion powder
1 tablespoon garlic powder
1 teaspoon cayenne pepper

Remove the membrane from the underside of the ribs. Prepare a heavy brine mixture of salt and water in a container large enough to hold the ribs. Add the ribs and soak for 24 hours in the refrigerator, making sure the ribs remain submerged. Drain the ribs and pat dry.

Whisk the paprika, black pepper, salt, chili powder, onion powder, garlic powder and cayenne pepper together in a bowl. Rub into the ribs, coating well. Arrange the ribs in a smoker. Smoke at 200 degrees for 3 hours or to the desired degree of doneness.

Serves 9

Apricot-Glazed Pork Roast

1 (10-ounce) can condensed
chicken broth
1 (18-ounce) jar apricot preserves
1 large onion, chopped
2 teaspoons Dijon mustard
1 (4-pound) boneless pork loin roast

Combine the broth, preserves, onion and Dijon mustard in a slow cooker. Add the pork, turning to coat. Cook on Low for 8 to 9 hours or until the pork is cooked through.

Slice and serve with the pan sauce.

Note: For a thicker sauce, remove the pork from the slow cooker. Mix 2 tablespoons cornstarch with 2 tablespoons water in a cup. Whisk into the pan sauce and cook on High for 10 minutes or until thickened.

Serves 8

Roasted Cuban Pork with Lime

1/3 cup fresh lime juice
3 large garlic cloves, chopped
1 tablespoon dried oregano
1 1/2 teaspoons salt
1/2 teaspoon pepper
4 pounds pork loin
Salt to taste

Combine the lime juice, garlic, oregano, 1 1/2 teaspoons salt and pepper in a large bowl and mix well. Add the pork, turning to coat. Marinate in the refrigerator for 8 to 10 hours, turning occasionally. Drain the marinade from the pork and let the pork come to room temperature. Season with salt. Roast, loosely covered with foil, in the center of your oven at 350 degrees for 1 hour. Uncover and roast for 1 1/2 hours longer. Let stand for 20 minutes before slicing to serve.

Serves 6

Mushroom Pork Tenderloin

2 (1-pound) pork tenderloins
1/4 cup mayonnaise
1 envelope onion soup mix
2 teaspoons minced garlic
8 ounces sliced baby portobellos
1 tablespoon all-purpose flour
1/2 cup milk

Slice each tenderloin diagonally into about twelve 1/2-inch slices. Combine the mayonnaise, soup mix and garlic in a large bowl. Add the mushrooms and pork and stir to coat well. Arrange in a preheated large sauté pan. Cook for 2 to 3 minutes per side or until browned. Whisk in the flour. Cook for 1 to 2 minutes. Stir in the milk and reduce the heat to low. Cook for 4 to 6 minutes or until the pork registers 160 degrees on a meat thermometer and the sauce is thickened.

Note: You may use venison tenderloin in place of the pork, if desired.

Serves 6

Pork Chile Verde with Cilantro Rice

1 pound pork tenderloin, cut into
    bite-size pieces
2 teaspoons ground cumin
1/2 teaspoon kosher salt
1/4 teaspoon pepper
2 teaspoons canola oil
4 cups coarsely chopped peeled
    tomatillos (about 10 to 12)
11/2 cups chopped onions
4 garlic cloves, coarsely chopped
1 tablespoon grated lime zest

2 tablespoons fresh lime juice
1 green bell pepper,
    coarsely chopped
1/2 teaspoon coarsely chopped
    jalapeño chile
1/2 cup coarsely chopped cilantro
1 (10-ounce) package frozen
    brown rice
1/2 cup coarsely chopped cilantro
1/4 teaspoon kosher salt
1/4 teaspoon pepper

Combine the pork, cumin, 1/2 teaspoon salt, 1/4 teaspoon pepper and 1 teaspoon of the canola oil in a large bowl and stir to coat the pork.

Heat a large stockpot over medium-high heat for 2 to 3 minutes. Add the pork and cook for 2 to 3 minutes or until browned on all sides. Add the remaining 1 teaspoon canola oil. Add the tomatillos, onions and garlic and cook for 3 to 4 minutes or until the onions are softened.

Stir in the lime zest and juice. Reduce the heat to medium-low and simmer, covered, for 60 to 65 minutes or until the pork is tender.

Stir in the bell pepper, jalapeño and 1/2 cup cilantro. Cook for 4 to 5 minutes longer or until the bell pepper is tender.

Prepare the rice according to the package directions. Stir in 1/2 cup cilantro, 1/4 teaspoon salt and 1/4 teaspoon pepper. Serve the pork over the rice.

Serves 4 to 6

Sausage and Pasta

8 ounces bow tie pasta or other small pasta
1 pound sausage links (about 5)
2 tablespoons olive oil
3 garlic cloves, minced
1 tablespoon chopped fresh or dried basil
1/4 teaspoon black pepper
1/4 teaspoon white pepper
1/4 teaspoon kosher salt
1 (6-ounce) can mushroom pieces
1 (15-ounce) can garbanzo beans, drained and rinsed
1 (15-ounce) can diced tomatoes
1 small banana pepper, cut into rings
1/2 cup (2 ounces) finely shredded Romano cheese

Cook the pasta according to the package directions; drain and keep warm. Grill the sausage until cooked through; let cool slightly, then thinly slice.

Heat the olive oil in a large skillet over medium heat. Add the garlic, basil, black pepper, white pepper and salt and mix well. Stir in the sausage, mushrooms, beans, tomatoes and banana pepper. Cook until heated through and bubbling. Stir the sausage mixture into the pasta in a large bowl. Sprinkle with the cheese and serve.

Serves 6

Forty-Clove Garlic Chicken with Monterey Rice

1 large whole chicken
3 tablespoons extra-virgin olive oil
40 large garlic cloves, peeled
1/2 cup white wine
1 teaspoon rosemary, crushed
1 teaspoon thyme
1 teaspoon ground ginger
1 bell pepper, chopped
8 ounces mushrooms, sliced
Butter
1 cup uncooked rice
Salt and pepper to taste

Clean the chicken and trim off any excess fat. Coat the chicken with the olive oil. Arrange the garlic in a slow cooker, reserving 3 or 4 cloves. Pour in the wine. Add the chicken, breast side up. Sprinkle the chicken with the rosemary, thyme and ginger. Arrange the reserved garlic around the chicken. Cook, covered, on Low for 8 to 10 hours or until the chicken is cooked through; do not remove the lid during cooking.

Sauté the bell pepper and mushrooms in a small amount of butter in a small skillet until softened. Cook the rice according to the package directions. Stir in the mushrooms, bell pepper, salt and pepper. Serve with the chicken.

Serves 6

Jennifer's Chicken Marsala

4 boneless skinless chicken breasts
Salt and pepper to taste
1 cup all-purpose flour
3 tablespoons butter
1 garlic clove, crushed
1 tablespoon butter
8 ounces sliced mushrooms
1/2 cup marsala
1/2 teaspoon salt

Pound the chicken on a work surface to 1/8- to 1/4-inch thickness. Season with salt and pepper. Dredge the chicken in the flour to coat. Melt 3 tablespoons butter in a skillet. Add the garlic and cook until light brown. Add the chicken and cook until brown on both sides, turning once.

Remove the chicken to a 9×13-inch baking dish that has been lightly coated with nonstick cooking spray, reserving the drippings in the skillet.

Add 1 tablespoon butter and the mushrooms to the reserved drippings. Cook until the mushrooms are light brown. Add the wine and bring to a boil. Simmer for 2 minutes to allow the flavors to blend. Pour the mushroom sauce over the chicken and sprinkle with 1/2 teaspoon salt. Bake, covered with foil, at 350 degrees for 30 minutes.

Serves 3 or 4

Easy Chicken Divan

2 tablespoons all-purpose flour
1 tablespoon seasoned salt
13/4 pounds chicken tenders
Butter for sautéing
3 cups broccoli florets
1 (15-ounce) jar light alfredo pasta sauce
1/4 cup white wine
3/4 cup (3 ounces) shredded Parmesan cheese

Combine the flour and seasoned salt in a large sealable plastic bag. Seal and shake to mix. Cut the chicken into bite-size pieces. Add to the flour mixture and shake to coat.

Heat a large sauté pan over medium-high heat for 2 to 3 minutes. Melt a small amount of butter in the pan. Add the chicken and cook for 4 to 5 minutes or until it begins to brown, stirring constantly. Add the broccoli. Cook, covered, for 4 to 5 minutes or until the broccoli is tender-crisp. Stir in the pasta sauce and wine.

Cook for 3 to 4 minutes or until the flavors have blended. Top with the cheese and serve hot.

Serves 4

Chicken Gertrude

2 pounds boneless chicken
2 cups water
1 teaspoon salt
Celery leaves
16 ounces mushrooms, sliced
Butter for sautéing
2 cups (8 ounces) shredded sharp
Cheddar cheese

2 cups cooked rice
1 cup blanched slivered almonds
3 tablespoons butter
3 tablespoons all-purpose flour
1 1/2 cups chicken broth
1 cup evaporated milk
1 teaspoon minced onion
1 teaspoon salt

Combine the chicken, water, 1 teaspoon salt and celery leaves in a saucepan and bring to a boil. Boil until the chicken is cooked through; drain. Cut the chicken into bite-size pieces.

Sauté the mushrooms in a small amount of butter in a small sauté pan until softened. Combine the chicken, mushrooms, cheese, rice and almonds in a large bowl and mix well. Spoon into a 2-quart baking dish.

Melt 3 tablespoons butter in a small saucepan. Whisk in the flour. Cook until thickened, stirring constantly. Whisk in the broth and evaporated milk gradually. Cook until thickened and of a sauce consistency, stirring frequently. Stir in the onion and 1 teaspoon salt. Pour over the chicken mixture in the baking dish. Bake at 350 degrees for 40 minutes.

Serves 6

Braised Chicken

4 skinless chicken breast quarters
4 skinless chicken leg quarters
3/4 teaspoon salt, or to taste
1/4 teaspoon freshly ground
   pepper, or to taste
5 tablespoons olive oil
5 garlic cloves, thinly sliced
1/4 cup white wine reduction
   (see Note)

30 picholine green olives
2 lemons, sliced 1/4 inch thick
2 bay leaves
3 cups chicken stock
Hot cooked rice
1/4 cup coarsely chopped
   fresh parsley

Season the chicken with the salt and pepper. Heat the olive oil in a large Dutch oven over medium-high heat. Add the chicken and cook until brown, working in batches if needed to prevent overcrowding. Remove the chicken to a plate, reserving the drippings in the pan.

Reduce the heat to medium and add the garlic. Cook for 15 to 20 seconds. Add the wine reduction and cook for 1 minute, scraping up the browned bits from the bottom of the pan. Add the olives, lemons and bay leaves and cook for about 2 minutes, stirring constantly. Return the chicken to the pan and immediately add the stock. Bring to a boil. Reduce the heat and simmer, covered, for about 2 hours or until the chicken is cooked through and very tender. Taste and adjust the seasonings, if desired. Serve over hot cooked rice and sprinkle with the parsley.

Note: To make White Wine Reduction, heat 3/4 cup white wine in a saucepan over low heat until reduced to 1/4 cup; do not simmer. Whisk in 1 tablespoon butter until melted.

Serves 8

Chunky Chicken Chili

6 tablespoons butter
1/4 cup olive oil
4 pounds boneless skinless chicken
breasts, cut into bite-size pieces
6 tablespoons butter
1/4 cup all-purpose flour
2 large onions, chopped
1 cup chopped red bell pepper
1 cup chopped green bell pepper
1 small jalapeño chile, seeded
and chopped
4 cups low-sodium chicken stock
2 cups heavy cream
Juice of 1/2 lime
2 (4-ounce) cans mild green chiles

4 fresh garlic cloves, minced
2 tablespoons kosher salt
2 tablespoons chili powder
1 tablespoon dried basil
1 tablespoon dried oregano
1 1/2 teaspoons coriander
1 1/2 teaspoons cumin
1 teaspoon cayenne pepper
1 teaspoon black pepper
2 (14-ounce) cans cannellini beans,
drained and rinsed
1/4 cup chopped cilantro
1 cup sour cream
1 cup (4 ounces) shredded
Cheddar cheese

Melt 6 tablespoons butter with the olive oil in a large Dutch oven over medium-high heat. Add the chicken and cook until brown and cooked through. Remove to a plate using a slotted spoon, reserving the drippings in the pan.

Melt 6 tablespoons butter with the drippings in the Dutch oven. Whisk in the flour. Cook until thickened, stirring constantly. Stir in the onions, bell peppers and jalapeño. Cook for 2 to 3 minutes. Add the stock, scraping up any browned bits from the bottom of the pan. Cook for 5 minutes or until the vegetables are softened. Stir in the cream.

Reduce the heat and cook until thickened, stirring occasionally. Add the lime juice, green chiles, garlic, salt, chili powder, basil, oregano, coriander, cumin, cayenne pepper and black pepper. Cook for 5 to 10 minutes, stirring and scraping the bottom of the pan frequently. Add the beans and cook for 5 to 8 minutes, stirring constantly. Stir in the cilantro and sour cream just before serving. To serve, ladle into bowls and top with the cheese.

Serves 8

Chicken Potpie

12 ounces boneless chicken breasts, cooked
1 (2-crust) refrigerator pie pastry
2 tablespoons butter
2 tablespoons all-purpose flour
1 teaspoon poultry seasoning
1 cup milk
1 (10-ounce) can cream of chicken soup
1 cup chicken broth
1 (10-ounce) package frozen chopped mixed vegetables
1 cup frozen pearl onions

Chop the chicken into bite-size pieces. Fit one of the pie pastries into a large circular baking dish, pressing around the edge and bottom. Poke holes all over the pastry with a fork. Bake at 450 degrees for 10 minutes or until light golden brown. Maintain the oven temperature.

Melt the butter in a large saucepan over medium heat. Whisk in the flour and poultry seasoning. Cook for 1 minute or until thickened, stirring constantly. Stir in the milk, soup and broth. Bring to a boil, stirring constantly. Add the chicken, mixed vegetables and onions. Reduce the heat to medium-low and cook for 10 minutes, stirring frequently.

Spoon the chicken mixture into the prepared crust. Top with the remaining pie pastry, trimming the edge and cutting a few slits in the top to vent. Bake for 10 minutes or until golden brown.

Note: Make sure you choose a baking dish large enough to accommodate all the ingredients. You may divide the filling between two pie plates; use four pie pastries if making two smaller potpies.

Serves 4 to 8

Hot Chicken Salad

1 (5-pound) bone-in chicken
2 packages croutons
2 cups sour cream
1¹/2 cups (or more) mayonnaise
8 ounces celery, chopped
4 carrots, shredded
1 onion, chopped
¹/2 cup (2 ounces) shredded Colby cheese
4 ounces sharp American cheese, shredded (Cooper's preferred)

Cook the chicken in water to cover in a stockpot until tender and falling from the bone; drain, reserving 1¹/2 cups of the broth. Pull the chicken from the bone and cut into large pieces.

Combine enough of the reserved broth with the croutons in a bowl to soften. Whisk the sour cream and mayonnaise in a bowl until blended. Combine the chicken, celery, carrots, onion, half the Colby cheese and half the American cheese in a large bowl and mix well. Stir in the croutons and enough of the mayonnaise mixture to reach a wet consistency. Spoon into two 9×13-inch baking dishes that have been well coated with nonstick cooking spray. Sprinkle the remaining cheese evenly over the tops. Bake, uncovered, at 350 degrees until bubbly.

Notes: To save time, you may use purchased chicken broth. You may also cook the chicken in a slow cooker on Low for 8 hours instead of boiling.

Serves 25

Wing Dings

1/2 cup soy sauce
1/2 cup water
1/2 cup sugar
1/4 cup pineapple juice
2 tablespoons vegetable oil
1/2 teaspoon garlic salt
1/2 teaspoon ginger
12 pieces chicken (wings, thighs or legs)

Whisk the soy sauce, water, sugar, pineapple juice, oil, garlic salt and ginger together in a bowl. Pour over the chicken in a shallow baking dish. Marinate in the refrigerator for 1 hour or longer. Bake, uncovered, at 375 degrees for 1 1/2 hours or until cooked through.

Serves 4 to 6

Back to the Garden

Chilled Marinated Asparagus

2/3 cup packed brown sugar
2/3 cup apple cider vinegar
2/3 cup soy sauce
2/3 cup vegetable oil
4 teaspoons lemon juice
1 teaspoon garlic powder
2 pounds fresh asparagus, trimmed
1 cup chopped pecans, toasted

Combine the brown sugar, vinegar, soy sauce, oil, lemon juice and garlic powder in a saucepan and bring to a boil. Reduce the heat and simmer, uncovered, for 5 minutes. Let cool slightly, then chill until cold.

Bring 1/2 inch water to a boil in a large skillet. Add the asparagus. Reduce the heat and simmer, covered, until tender-crisp; drain. Rinse in cold water to stop the cooking process. Combine the asparagus and brown sugar mixture in a large sealable plastic bag, turning to coat. Chill for 2 to 10 hours, turning occasionally.

Drain and discard the marinade. Arrange the asparagus on a serving plate. Sprinkle with the pecans and serve cold.

Serves 4

Roasted Brussels Sprouts

1 1/2 pounds brussels sprouts
3 tablespoons olive oil
3/4 cup walnuts

Trim the ends from the brussels sprouts and cut each into halves. Pour the olive oil into a large skillet. Add the brussels sprouts and walnuts. Cook over medium-high heat until roasted and brown, stirring constantly.

Serves 6

Hot Irish Potato and Cabbage Salad

8 to 10 potatoes, cooked and mashed
2 cups shredded cabbage
1/4 cup chopped onion
1 cup sour cream
8 ounces cream cheese, softened
1/2 cup (1 stick) butter or margarine, melted
1 garlic clove, minced
2 teaspoons salt
1 tablespoon parsley flakes

Combine the hot mashed potatoes, cabbage, onion, sour cream, cream cheese, butter, garlic, salt and parsley in a large bowl and mix well. Spoon into a 9×13-inch baking dish coated with nonstick cooking spray. Bake at 350 degrees for 40 minutes or until heated through. Garnish with additional parsley flakes before serving.

Serves 10 to 12

Yard House Barbecue Beans

1/4 cup olive oil
1 cup chopped green onions
2 tablespoons minced garlic
1 or 2 small jalapeño chiles, seeded and minced
4 cups cooked pinto beans (see Note)
2 cups chicken broth
1 cup packed brown sugar
1 cup barbecue sauce
2 to 4 tablespoons puréed chipotle chiles in adobo sauce
2 teaspoons Tabasco sauce
Salt and pepper to taste

Heat a medium heavy-bottomed stockpot over medium-high heat until hot. Add the olive oil, green onions, garlic and jalapeño. Sauté for about 2 minutes or until the garlic is golden brown and aromatic, stirring constantly. Stir in the beans, broth, brown sugar, barbecue sauce, chipotle chile purée and Tabasco sauce. Bring to a boil, stirring frequently to prevent burning.

Reduce the heat and simmer for 15 to 20 minutes or just until the beans begin to break apart. Taste and adjust the spices and seasonings as desired. Mash some of the beans with the back of a spoon against the side of the stockpot and stir to thicken. Store any leftovers, covered, in the refrigerator for up to 4 days.

Note: For the beans, cook 1 pound dried pinto beans, reserving the cooking liquid to use in place of the broth, if desired. To save time, you may substitute three 15-ounce cans pinto beans that have been drained and rinsed.

Serves 6 to 8

Gigi's Sweet Potato Soufflé

4 cups mashed cooked sweet potatoes
2 medium eggs
1 1/2 cups granulated sugar
1 cup milk
1/4 cup (1/2 stick) butter, melted
1 teaspoon vanilla extract
1/2 teaspoon salt
1/2 teaspoon baking powder
1/2 teaspoon lemon juice
1/4 teaspoon nutmeg
1 cup packed brown sugar
1/2 cup all-purpose flour
1/3 cup butter, melted
1 cup chopped pecans

Beat the sweet potatoes, eggs, granulated sugar, milk, 1/4 cup butter and vanilla in a large bowl until blended. Add the salt, baking powder, lemon juice and nutmeg and mix well. Spoon into a greased baking dish. Bake at 350 degrees for 20 to 25 minutes or until heated through.

Combine the brown sugar, flour, 1/3 cup butter and pecans in a bowl and mix until crumbly. Sprinkle over the soufflé and bake for 15 minutes longer.

Serves 6

Sweet Potato Casserole

2¹/2 pounds fresh sweet potatoes,
or 2 (29-ounce) cans sweet potatoes
¹/2 cup (1 stick) unsalted butter or
margarine, cut into pieces
¹/3 cup granulated sugar
¹/4 cup packed brown sugar
Dash of honey
1 teaspoon vanilla extract
³/4 teaspoon salt
¹/3 teaspoon grated nutmeg
2 eggs, lightly beaten
1¹/4 cups milk, heated
Sugar and Spice Topping (page 127)

Arrange the sweet potatoes on a rimmed baking sheet. Bake at 350 degrees for 1¹/2 hours or until tender. Let cool for 10 minutes, then peel. Beat the sweet potatoes in a large bowl at low speed until mashed. Beat in the butter. Add the granulated sugar, brown sugar, honey, vanilla, salt and nutmeg and mix well. Add the eggs and beat at medium speed for 2 minutes. Beat in the hot milk gradually at low speed until blended. Spoon into a buttered 9×13-inch baking dish and spread in an even layer. Sprinkle the topping over the sweet potato mixture.

Bake at 375 degrees for 1¹/4 hours or until the topping is light brown and crisp. If the topping browns too quickly, cover loosely with a sheet of foil that has a hole cut out of the center.

Note: The sweet potato mixture and topping can be made 1 day in advance and stored separately in the refrigerator.

Serves 24

Sugar and Spice Topping

1/2 cup all-purpose flour
1/2 cup packed light brown sugar
1/4 teaspoon cinnamon
1/4 teaspoon grated nutmeg

1/4 teaspoon salt
1/4 cup (1/2 stick) unsalted butter,
    cut into pieces and chilled
1/2 cup chopped pecans

Combine the flour, brown sugar, cinnamon, nutmeg and salt in a bowl and mix well. Cut in the cold butter until the mixture resembles coarse meal. Stir in the pecans.

Easy Sweet Potato Casserole

2 eggs
3/4 cup granulated sugar
1/3 cup milk
1/2 cup (1 stick) butter, softened
1 teaspoon vanilla extract
1 (29-ounce) can sweet potatoes,
    heated and mashed

1 cup packed brown sugar
1/2 cup all-purpose flour
1 cup chopped nuts
3/4 cup (11/2 sticks) butter,
    softened

Beat the eggs, granulated sugar, milk, 1/2 cup butter and vanilla in a bowl until blended and creamy. Mix in the sweet potatoes. Spoon into a greased 2-quart baking dish. Mix the brown sugar, flour, nuts and 3/4 cup butter in a bowl until crumbly. Sprinkle over the sweet potato mixture. Bake at 350 degrees for 35 minutes.

Serves 4

Creamed Spinach

10 ounces fresh spinach
1 to 2 (14-ounce) cans chicken broth
8 ounces cream cheese, softened
8 ounces mozzarella cheese, shredded

Salt and pepper to taste
Minced garlic or garlic salt to taste
All-natural seasoning to taste
  (such as Spike)

Cook the spinach in the broth in a saucepan until wilted; drain. Stir in the cream cheese. Stir in the mozzarella cheese until melted. Season with salt, pepper, garlic and all-natural seasoning. Serve hot.

Serves 6 to 8

Zucchini Pie

1 cup baking mix
4 eggs, beaten
1/4 cup vegetable oil
1 teaspoon parsley flakes
1/2 teaspoon salt

1/4 teaspoon pepper
3 cups sliced zucchini
1 small onion, thinly sliced
1/2 cup (2 ounces) grated Parmesan
  cheese or shredded Cheddar cheese

Beat the baking mix, eggs, oil, parsley, salt and pepper together in a bowl. Stir in the zucchini, onion and cheese. Spoon into a 9-inch pie plate coated with nonstick cooking spray. Bake at 350 degrees for 35 minutes. Let stand for about 5 minutes before slicing to serve.

Serves 8

Vegetarian Delight

2 tablespoons olive oil
2 onions, sliced
1 handful sesame seeds
16 ounces fresh mushrooms, sliced
1 to 1 1/2 pounds zucchini, sliced
4 large firm tomatoes, chopped
Salt and pepper to taste
1 cup pitted black olives, sliced
1 cup (4 ounces) shredded
Monterey Jack cheese

Heat the olive oil in a large skillet. Add the onions and sesame seeds and sauté for several minutes or until golden brown. Layer some of the mushrooms, zucchini and tomatoes over the onions. Season with salt and pepper. Top with the remaining mushrooms, zucchini and tomatoes. Scatter the olives evenly over the top. Cook, uncovered, over low heat for 20 to 25 minutes or until the vegetables are tender-crisp. Sprinkle the cheese over the top and heat until the cheese melts. Serve hot or cold.

Note: You may cook as directed above, using an ovenproof skillet. After adding the cheese, heat under a broiler until golden brown.

Serves 6

Jeanni's Eggplant Parmesan

Eggplant

3 eggplant, trimmed

1 tablespoon sea salt

3 eggs

1 teaspoon sea salt

1 cup all-purpose flour

2 cups seasoned bread crumbs

1 cup olive oil or grapeseed oil

2 cups (8 ounces) freshly grated Parmesan cheese

12 leaves fresh basil, thinly sliced

16 ounces fresh mozzarella or fontina cheese, shredded

Sea salt and freshly ground pepper to taste

Tomato Gravy

1 large onion, chopped

2 tablespoons extra-virgin olive oil

4 garlic cloves (or more to taste), minced

6 to 8 ounces tomato paste

2 (28-ounce) cans crushed Italian tomatoes, or 3 1/2 pounds fresh tomatoes, peeled

1 tomato can of water

1/4 cup extra-virgin olive oil

1/2 cup red wine

1 cup pitted olives, chopped

1 cup chopped fresh basil and oregano

Sea salt and freshly ground pepper to taste

For the eggplant, cut each eggplant into eight 1/2-inch slices. Sprinkle with 1 tablespoon salt and let drain in a colander for 1 hour; rinse and pat dry.

Whisk the eggs with 1 teaspoon salt in a shallow bowl. Place the flour in another bowl and spread the bread crumbs on a plate. Dredge the eggplant in the flour, shaking off any excess. Dip into the egg mixture, then press into the bread crumbs to coat. Heat 1/2 cup of the olive oil in a large skillet. Fry the eggplant in the hot oil in batches over medium-high heat, adding additional olive oil as needed and turning once to brown both sides. Remove to a paper towel-lined plate to drain.

For the gravy, sauté the onion in 2 tablespoons olive oil in a stockpot for 2 to 3 minutes. Add the garlic and sauté for 1 minute. Stir in the tomato paste and cook for 10 minutes. Stir in the tomatoes and water. Bring to a boil and add 1/4 cup olive oil. Stir in the wine, olives, herbs, salt and pepper. Reduce the heat and simmer, uncovered, for 1 hour or longer, stirring occasionally.

To assemble and bake, ladle enough of the gravy to coat the bottom into a greased 9×13-inch baking dish. Sprinkle lightly with some of the Parmesan cheese. Top with an even layer of the fried eggplant and sprinkle with one-third of the basil. Season with salt and pepper. Ladle about 3/4 cup of the gravy over the layers and sprinkle lightly with Parmesan cheese. Top with one-third of the mozzarella cheese. Repeat the layers twice, ending with the mozzarella cheese. Drizzle with the remaining gravy and Parmesan cheese.

Cover the baking dish loosely with foil and poke a few holes to vent. Bake at 350 degrees for 30 minutes. Uncover and bake for 15 minutes longer or until golden brown in places. Let stand for several minutes before cutting into squares to serve.

Serves 8 to 12

Lisle's Tomato Gravy

2 tablespoons butter
1 tablespoon olive oil
1/4 cup finely chopped onion
1 garlic clove, minced
1/4 cup all-purpose flour
3 large ripe tomatoes, peeled, seeded
and chopped
1/2 teaspoon sea salt
1/2 teaspoon cracked black pepper
Pinch of cayenne pepper
1 cup (or more) half-and-half

Melt the butter with the olive oil in a large saucepan over medium heat. Add the onion and garlic and sauté until aromatic, watching closely to prevent burning. Increase the heat and whisk in the flour. Cook until thickened, stirring constantly. Add the tomatoes, crushing them with the back of a spoon until very soft. Cook for 5 minutes longer, stirring constantly. Season with the salt, black pepper and cayenne pepper. Add the half-and-half. Cook until heated through, stirring constantly. Add additional half-and-half if a thinner consistency is desired. Serve on anything.

Makes about 2 cups

Wild Rice and Vegetables with Balsamic Vinegar

1 cup wild rice, rinsed
3 cups water
1 tablespoon olive oil
1 onion, chopped
1 large zucchini, chopped
1 cup fresh mushrooms, sliced
1 (17-ounce) jar roasted red peppers, drained and sliced
1 large tomato, sliced
3 tablespoons balsamic vinegar
Salt and pepper to taste

Bring the rice and water to a boil in a medium saucepan. Reduce the heat and simmer, covered, for 8 to 10 minutes or until the rice is tender. Heat the olive oil in a skillet and add the onion, zucchini and mushrooms. Sauté for 5 minutes, stirring frequently. Remove from the heat and let cool slightly. Add the roasted red peppers, tomato and vinegar. Combine the rice and vegetable mixture in a large bowl and toss to mix. Season with salt and pepper and serve.

Serves 8

Oven Rice

1/4 cup (1/2 stick) butter
1 1/2 cups white rice
1 (4-ounce) can mushrooms stems and pieces

1 (10-ounce) can beef consommé
1 (10-ounce) can French onion soup
1 (8-ounce) can water chestnuts (optional)

Melt the butter in a 3-quart stovetop-safe baking dish over medium heat. Add the rice and sauté for several minutes to coat. Stir in the mushrooms, consommé, onion soup and water chestnuts. Bake, covered, at 350 degrees for 1 hour.

Serves 6

Yummy Macaroni and Cheese

2 cups macaroni
Salt to taste
1/2 cup (1 stick) margarine

2 cups milk
2 eggs, beaten
16 ounces sharp cheese, shredded

Cook the pasta in boiling salted water in a stockpot until tender; drain. Stir the margarine into the hot pasta until melted. Add the milk, eggs and cheese and mix well. Spoon into a 9×13-inch baking dish. Bake at 300 degrees for 30 minutes or until golden brown.

Serves 10

Elsie's Turkey Stuffing

1 pound bulk pork sausage (Bob Evans preferred)
1¹/₂ packages plain croutons
4 ribs celery, chopped
4 carrots, chopped
2 large onions, chopped
3 tablespoons parsley flakes
1 tablespoon poultry seasoning
1¹/₂ teaspoons salt
¹/₄ teaspoon pepper
1¹/₄ cups hot water
1 (13-pound) turkey, seasoned as desired
¹/₂ to 1 cup (1 to 2 sticks) butter

Brown the sausage in a large skillet, stirring until crumbly. Remove the sausage to a large bowl using a slotted spoon, reserving the drippings in the skillet. Add the croutons to the sausage and mix well.

Add the celery, carrots and onions to the drippings in the skillet and sauté until slightly softened. Spoon over the sausage mixture. Add the parsley, poultry seasoning, salt and pepper to the sausage mixture and mix well. Add the hot water and stir to coat all ingredients evenly. Cover and chill the stuffing for 8 to 10 hours.

Spoon the stuffing into the turkey cavities. Pour the butter over the stuffing in the turkey. Cook the turkey according to the package directions or using your favorite recipe. When the turkey tests done, remove the stuffing to a serving bowl and serve alongside the sliced turkey.

Note: The stuffing recipe can be easily doubled. Spoon any stuffing that doesn't fit in the turkey into a baking dish. Dot with butter and bake at 350 degrees for about 1 hour or until the vegetables are soft.

Serves 6 to 8

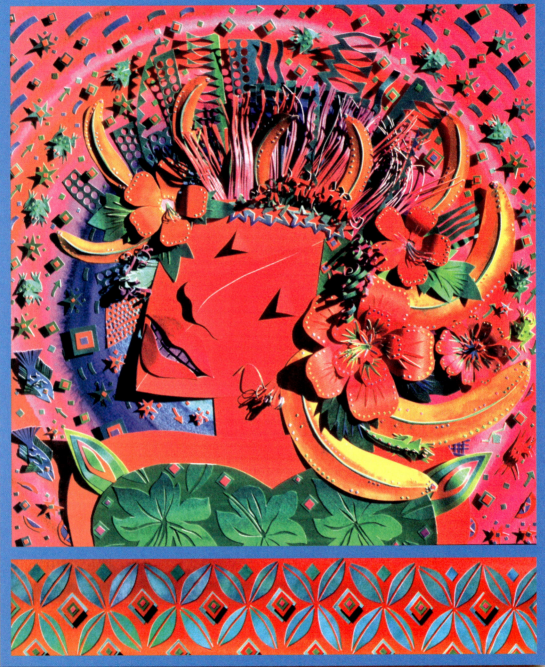

Just Desserts

Almond Skillet Cake

3/4 cup (1¹/₂ sticks) unsalted butter, melted
1¹/₂ cups sugar
2 eggs
1¹/₂ cups all-purpose flour
1 teaspoon almond extract
Dash of salt
Slivered almonds to taste
Sugar for sprinkling

Line a cast-iron skillet with foil. Spray the foil generously with nonstick cooking spray. Cream the butter and sugar in a large bowl. Add the eggs, flour, almond extract and salt and mix well. Pour into the prepared skillet. Sprinkle with slivered almonds and additional sugar. Bake at 350 degrees for 30 minutes.

Serves 4 to 6

Blackberry Wine Cake

Glaze
1/2 cup (1 stick) butter or margarine
1/3 cup confectioners' sugar
1/2 cup blackberry wine

Cake
1/2 cup chopped pecans
1 (2-layer) package white cake mix
1 (3-ounce) package blackberry gelatin
4 eggs
1/2 cup blackberry wine
1/2 cup vegetable oil

For the glaze, heat the butter and confectioners' sugar in a small saucepan over low heat until melted, stirring frequently until blended. Remove from the heat and whisk in the wine. Keep warm.

For the cake, spray a bundt pan with nonstick bakers' spray. Sprinkle the pecans over the bottom of the prepared pan. Combine the cake mix, gelatin, eggs, wine and oil in a bowl and beat at medium speed for 2 minutes. Pour the batter evenly over the pecans. Bake at 325 degrees for 50 minutes or until the cake tests done.

While the cake is still warm and in the pan, poke holes all over the cake using a fork. Pour 1/3 of the glaze over the cake and let cool for 30 minutes. Turn the cake onto a serving plate. Poke holes all over the cake using a fork. Spoon the remainder of the glaze over the cake.

Serves 8 to 12

Triple Chocolate Cake

1 (2-layer) package devil's food cake mix
1 large package cook-and-serve
chocolate pudding mix
1/2 cup brewed coffee
4 eggs, beaten

1 cup sour cream
1/2 cup vegetable oil
1/2 cup coffee liqueur
1 (12-ounce) package semisweet
chocolate chips

Coat a bundt pan with nonstick bakers' spray. Combine the cake mix and pudding mix in a bowl and mix well. Stir in the coffee. Add the eggs, sour cream, oil, liqueur and chocolate chips one ingredient at a time, mixing well after each addition. Pour the batter into the prepared pan. Bake at 350 degrees for 60 to 70 minutes or until the cake tests done.

Serves 10 to 12

Five-Minute Chocolate Mug Cake

1/4 cup all-purpose flour
1/4 cup sugar
2 tablespoons baking cocoa
1 egg

3 tablespoons milk
3 tablespoons vegetable oil
3 tablespoons chocolate chips (optional)
1/2 teaspoon vanilla extract

Combine the flour, sugar and baking cocoa in a large mug and mix well. Add the egg and mix thoroughly. Add the milk and oil and mix well. Stir in the chocolate chips and vanilla. Place the mug in the microwave and heat on High for 3 minutes. (The cake may rise slightly out of the mug.) Let cool slightly.

Enjoy from the mug or tip onto a plate.

Serves 1 or 2

Hershey's Chocolate Cake

1 (2-layer) package white cake mix
1 (4-ounce) package vanilla instant
pudding mix
4 eggs
3/4 cup vegetable oil

1 cup water
1 (6-ounce) package miniature
chocolate chips
2/3 cup Hershey's chocolate syrup

Beat the cake mix, pudding mix, eggs, oil and water in a bowl until blended. Pour 2/3 of the batter into a greased and floured bundt pan. Sprinkle half the chocolate chips over the top. Stir the chocolate syrup into the remaining batter. Pour over the layers in the pan. Sprinkle with the remaining chocolate chips. Swirl the batter lightly with a knife. Bake at 350 degrees for 50 minutes or until the cake tests done.

Serves 10

Sunsets

Island sunsets can only be described as breathtaking!

Standing on St. George's Island
Every voice and penciled shell
Bending with the Ocean's music
Seemed to me a story tell.
And the love of every lover
Seemed to speak in love to me—
When I saw the golden sunset
Sinking o'er the Florida sea.

Mom's Chocolate Oatmeal Cake

Coconut Almond Frosting

1/2 cup (1 stick) butter
1 cup half-and-half or evaporated milk
1 cup packed light brown sugar

1 teaspoon pure vanilla extract
2 cups shredded sweetened coconut
1 cup sliced or chopped almonds

Cake

1 1/3 cups boiling water
1 cup quick-cooking oats
1 1/2 cups all-purpose flour
2 tablespoons baking cocoa
1 teaspoon baking soda
1 teaspoon fragrant ground cinnamon
1/2 teaspoon salt
1/2 cup (1 stick) salted butter, softened

1 cup packed light brown sugar
1 cup granulated sugar
2 eggs
2 teaspoons pure vanilla extract
1/4 teaspoon almond extract
1 cup raisins or dried cranberries
(optional)

For the frosting, melt the butter with the half-and-half in a saucepan over low heat. Let stand until 5 minutes before the cake will be finished baking. Add the brown sugar and vanilla. Bring to a full boil and cook for 4 to 5 minutes, whisking constantly. Stir in the coconut and almonds.

For the cake, pour the boiling water over the oats in a heatproof bowl. Let stand for 20 minutes. Sift the flour, baking cocoa, baking soda, cinnamon and salt together twice. Beat the butter with the brown sugar and granulated sugar in a bowl until fluffy and creamy. Beat in the eggs. Add the vanilla, almond extract, oats and raisins and mix well. Stir in the sifted ingredients. Beat at low speed until blended. Pour into a lightly greased and floured 9×11-inch cake pan. Bake at 350 degrees for 40 to 50 minutes or until the cake tests done. Remove from the oven and gently poke holes over the top of the cake using a fork. Spread the Coconut Almond Frosting evenly over the cake. Broil for 2 minutes or until light brown, watching carefully to prevent burning.

Serves 24

Rave Reviews Coconut Cake

Coconut Cream Cheese Frosting

2 tablespoons butter or margarine

2 cups flaked coconut

2 tablespoons butter or margarine, softened

8 ounces cream cheese, softened

2 teaspoons milk

3¹/2 cups sifted confectioners' sugar

1/2 teaspoon vanilla extract

Cake

1 (2-layer) package yellow cake mix

1 small package vanilla instant pudding mix

1¹/3 cups water

4 eggs

1/4 cup vegetable oil

2 cups flaked coconut

1 cup walnuts or pecans

For the frosting, melt 2 tablespoons butter in a skillet. Add the coconut and cook over low heat until golden brown, stirring constantly. Spread the coconut on a paper towel to cool. Beat 2 tablespoons butter with the cream cheese in a bowl until creamy. Beat in the milk. Beat in the confectioners' sugar gradually until creamy and of spreading consistency. Beat in the vanilla. Stir in 1³/4 cups of the toasted coconut, reserving the remaining 1/4 cup for the assembly.

For the cake, combine the cake mix, pudding mix, water, eggs and oil in a large bowl and beat at medium speed for 4 minutes. Stir in the coconut and walnuts. Pour the batter evenly into 3 greased and floured 9-inch cake pans. Bake at 350 degrees for 35 minutes or until the layers test done. Let cool in the pans for 15 minutes. Remove to a wire rack to cool completely. Spread Coconut Cream Cheese Frosting between the layers and over the top of the cake. Sprinkle with the reserved 1/4 cup toasted coconut.

Serves 10 to 12

Lazy Daisy Cake

Coconut Topping

3 tablespoons butter, melted
3 tablespoons heavy cream
6 tablespoons brown sugar
1/2 cup shredded coconut

Cake

2 tablespoons butter, melted
1/2 cup milk
1 cup sugar
2 eggs, beaten
1 teaspoon vanilla extract
1 cup all-purpose flour
1 teaspoon baking powder
1/4 teaspoon salt

For the topping, combine the butter, cream, brown sugar and coconut in a bowl and mix well.

For the cake, combine the butter and milk in a small saucepan. Heat until just below the boiling point; set aside. Beat the sugar, eggs and vanilla in a bowl until creamy. Whisk the flour, baking powder and salt together in a small bowl. Stir into the creamed mixture. Add the scalded milk mixture quickly and stir rapidly until smooth. Pour the batter into a buttered 9×9-inch cake pan. Bake at 350 degrees for 35 minutes or until the cake tests done. Spread the Coconut Topping over the top. Broil until the topping is light brown.

Serves 12

Lemon Lovers' Cake

Lemon Glaze
1 cup confectioners' sugar
3 tablespoons lemon juice

Lemon Cake
1 (3-ounce) package lemon gelatin
1 cup boiling water
1 (2-layer) package lemon supreme cake mix
4 eggs
3/4 cup vegetable oil
1/2 teaspoon lemon extract

For the glaze, whisk the confectioners' sugar and lemon juice together in a bowl until smooth.

For the cake, dissolve the gelatin in the boiling water in a small heatproof bowl. Combine the cake mix, eggs and oil in a mixing bowl and beat until blended. Beat in the gelatin mixture and lemon extract. Pour into a greased and floured bundt pan. Bake at 325 degrees for 1 hour or until the cake tests done. Let cool for 15 to 20 minutes. Invert onto a serving plate. Drizzle the Lemon Glaze over the warm cake.

Serves 10 to 12

Chocolate Cream Cheese Pound Cake

Chocolate Frosting
1 cup sugar
1/4 cup baking cocoa
1/4 cup (or more) milk
1/4 cup (1/2 stick) butter, melted
1/2 teaspoon vanilla extract
Dash of salt

Cake
11/2 cups (3 sticks) butter, softened
8 ounces cream cheese, softened
3 cups sugar
6 eggs
1/2 cup baking cocoa
3 cups all-purpose flour
1 teaspoon vanilla extract
1 cup chopped pecans
1/2 cup finely chopped pecans

For the frosting, combine the sugar, baking cocoa, milk, butter, vanilla and salt in a saucepan. Cook over medium heat for 11/2 minutes, stirring frequently. Let cool to spreading consistency. Add additional milk if the frosting is too thick.

For the cake, cream the butter, cream cheese and sugar in a large bowl until fluffy. Add the eggs one at a time, beating after each addition. Sift the baking cocoa with the flour. Add to the creamed mixture gradually. Stir in the vanilla and 1 cup pecans. Pour into a greased tube pan. Bake at 325 degrees for 11/2 hours or until the cake tests done. Remove to a wire rack and let cool completely. Spread the Chocolate Frosting over the top and side of the cake. Sprinkle the top with 1/2 cup pecans.

Serves 10 to 12

Double Peanut Butter Pound Cake

Peanut Butter Frosting
1/2 cup creamy peanut butter
1/2 cup light corn syrup
2 cups confectioners' sugar
1 tablespoon milk
1 teaspoon vanilla extract

Cake
3 cups all-purpose flour
1/2 teaspoon baking powder
1/2 teaspoon salt
1 cup (2 sticks) butter, softened
3/4 cup creamy peanut butter
3 cups sugar
2 teaspoons vanilla extract
5 eggs
1 cup milk

For the frosting, melt the peanut butter with the corn syrup in a saucepan over low heat, stirring frequently. Stir in the confectioners' sugar, milk and vanilla until smooth. Remove from the heat and keep warm.

For the cake, sift the flour, baking powder and salt together. Beat the butter, peanut butter, sugar and vanilla in a large bowl until creamy and blended. Add the eggs one at a time, beating well after each addition. Add the flour mixture alternately with the milk, mixing well after each addition. Pour into a greased and floured tube pan. Bake at 350 degrees for 11/4 hours or until the cake tests done. Cool in the pan for 10 to 15 minutes. Invert onto a serving plate. Drizzle the Peanut Butter Frosting all over the cake.

Serves 12

My Granny's Pound Cake

3 cups all-purpose flour
1 tablespoon baking powder
1/2 teaspoon salt
1 cup (2 sticks) butter, softened
3 cups sugar
6 eggs
1 cup sour cream
1 tablespoon vanilla extract

Coat a 9- or 10-inch tube pan with butter and dust with flour. Sift 3 cups flour, baking powder and salt together. Beat the butter and sugar together in a bowl until creamy. Add the eggs one at a time, beating well after each addition. Fold in the flour mixture alternately with the sour cream, mixing well after each addition. Stir in the vanilla. Pour evenly into the prepared pan. Bake at 330 degrees for 11/2 hours or until the cake tests done.

Note: This pound cake gets even better the second day. Toast slices and top with butter and tropical marmalade or fruit conserve.

Serves 24

Sour Cream Pound Cake

3 cups all-purpose flour
1/4 teaspoon baking soda
1 1/2 cups (3 sticks) butter, softened
3 cups sugar
6 eggs
1 cup sour cream
1 teaspoon vanilla extract
1/2 teaspoon almond extract

Sift the flour and baking soda together three times. Beat the butter with the sugar in a mixing bowl until creamy and fluffy. Beat in the eggs one at a time, beating well after each addition. Add the flour mixture alternately with the sour cream, mixing well after each addition. Stir in the vanilla and almond extract. Pour into a greased and floured tube pan. Bake at 300 degrees for 75 to 80 minutes or until the cake tests done. Serve topped with chocolate glaze and/or chopped walnuts.

Serves 12

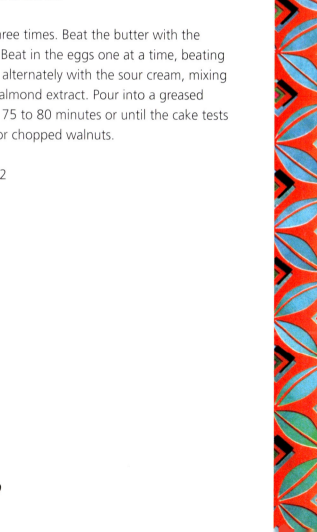

Tres Leches Cake

1 1/2 cups all-purpose flour
2 1/2 teaspoons baking powder
5 egg whites
Pinch of cream of tartar
1 cup sugar
5 egg yolks
1/4 cup milk
1 cup coconut milk
1 (5-ounce) can evaporated milk
1 (14-ounce) can sweetened condensed milk
Toasted coconut

Sift the flour and baking powder together. Combine the egg whites and cream of tartar in a large clean bowl. Beat at medium speed until soft peaks form. Beat in the sugar gradually at high speed. Beat in the egg yolks one at a time. Fold in the flour mixture alternately with the milk. Stir just until combined. Pour into a lightly greased 9×13-inch cake pan, smoothing the top. Bake at 350 degrees for 30 minutes or until the cake tests done. Let cool for 10 minutes.

Combine the coconut milk, evaporated milk and sweetened condensed milk in a bowl and mix well. Poke holes in the cake in the pan at 1-inch intervals. Pour the milk mixture over the top, making sure to moisten the edges and corners.

Let cool completely. Chill for 3 hours or longer. Cut into squares and top with toasted coconut to serve.

Serves 12

Sweet Cherry Cheese Pie

8 ounces cream cheese, softened
$1/4$ cup sour cream
$1/3$ teaspoon grated lemon zest
1 (9-inch) graham cracker pie crust
2 cups pitted cherries
$1/2$ cup sugar
2 tablespoons fresh lemon juice
1 cup water
3 tablespoons cornstarch

Beat the cream cheese, sour cream and lemon zest in a bowl until blended. Spoon evenly into the crust. Cover with waxed paper, pressing lightly onto the surface, and chill.

Combine the cherries, sugar, lemon juice and water in a heavy saucepan over medium heat and bring to a boil. Drain, reserving the cherries and cooking liquid separately. Pour $1 1/4$ cups of the cooking liquid into a small saucepan. Sprinkle the cornstarch over the top and whisk to combine. Bring to a boil over medium heat and cook until thickened, whisking constantly. Stir in the cherries. Let stand until cool. Pour over the cream cheese layer. Chill for 1 hour or until set.

Serves 6 to 8

Chocolate Pie

2¹/₂ cups milk
3 ounces unsweetened chocolate
1 cup sugar
6 tablespoons all-purpose flour
¹/₂ teaspoon salt
2 egg yolks
2 tablespoons butter
1 teaspoon vanilla extract
1 baked (9-inch) pie shell

Combine the milk and chocolate in the top of a double boiler set over simmering water. Heat until the chocolate melts, stirring constantly. Combine the sugar, flour and salt in a bowl. Stir in enough of the chocolate mixture to moisten the dry ingredients. Stir the sugar mixture gradually into the milk mixture. Cook until thickened, stirring constantly. Cook for 10 minutes longer, stirring constantly. Whisk the egg yolks in a bowl. Whisk a small amount of the hot mixture into the eggs, then whisk the eggs into the hot mixture. Cook for 2 minutes. Remove from the heat and stir in the butter and vanilla. Let cool, then pour into the pie shell. Chill until serving time.

Note: To make a meringue topping, beat 2 egg whites in a bowl until soft peaks form. Beat in ¹/₄ cup sugar and ¹/₈ teaspoon cream of tartar gradually until stiff peaks form. Spread over the top of the warm filling, spreading the meringue all the way to the edge. Bake at 350 degrees for 15 minutes or until light brown. Let cool completely, then store in the refrigerator until serving time.

Serves 8

Chocolate Chip Pecan Pie

1 (9-inch) refrigerator pie pastry
1/2 cup (1 stick) butter, softened
1 cup (about) sugar
2 eggs
1/3 cup cornstarch
1 teaspoon vanilla extract
1 (12-ounce) package chocolate chips
1 cup chopped pecans

Fit the pie pastry into a 9-inch pie plate, trimming and fluting the edge. Beat the butter and sugar in a bowl until blended and creamy. Add the eggs one at a time, beating well after each addition. Add the cornstarch and vanilla and beat well. Stir in the chocolate chips and pecans. Pour into the pie pastry. Bake at 375 degrees for 45 minutes. Let cool completely before serving.

Serves 8

Mary Frances's Bourbon Chocolate Pie

2 eggs
1 cup sugar
1/2 teaspoon salt
1/2 cup (1 stick) butter
1 (6-ounce) package chocolate chips
1/2 cup all-purpose flour
1 tablespoon bourbon
1 cup chopped nuts (optional)
1 unbaked (9-inch) pie shell

Beat the eggs and sugar together in a bowl until blended and creamy. Beat in the salt. Heat the butter and chocolate chips together in a small saucepan until melted, stirring occasionally. Remove from the heat and stir in the flour and bourbon. Add the chocolate mixture to the egg mixture and mix well. Stir in the nuts. Pour into the pie shell. Bake at 350 degrees for 1 hour.

Serves 6 to 8

Easy Coconut Cream Pie

1 (9-inch) refrigerator pie pastry
1¹/2 cups sugar
¹/2 cup cornstarch
4 egg yolks
3 cups milk
2 tablespoons butter
1 teaspoon vanilla extract

¹/2 cup shredded coconut
4 egg whites
1 teaspoon cream of tartar
1 tablespoon cornstarch
¹/2 cup sugar
Additional shredded coconut

Fit the pie pastry into a 9-inch pie plate, trimming and fluting the edge. Bake according to the package directions; let cool completely.

Whisk 1¹/2 cups sugar with ¹/2 cup cornstarch in a bowl. Whisk the egg yolks and milk together in a 2-quart microwave-safe bowl. Whisk in the sugar mixture. Microwave for 3¹/2 minutes; whisk. Microwave for 3 minutes longer; whisk again. Microwave once more for 3 minutes; remove and whisk to mix. Microwave for 1 to 2 minutes longer if needed to reach a thick custard consistency. Stir in the butter, vanilla and ¹/2 cup coconut. Pour into the prepared pie shell.

Beat the egg whites in a bowl until soft peaks form. Add the cream of tartar, 1 tablespoon cornstarch and ¹/2 cup sugar gradually, beating constantly until stiff peaks form. Spread the meringue over the filling, sealing to the edge. Sprinkle with coconut. Bake at 350 degrees for 10 to 15 minutes or until light brown on top.

Serves 12

Juanita's Key Lime Pie

1 cup shortbread cookies
1/2 cup macadamia nuts
5 tablespoons butter, melted
1/4 cup sugar
4 egg yolks (see Note)
1 (14-ounce) can sweetened condensed milk
8 ounces cream cheese, softened
1/2 cup Key lime juice
1 cup whipped cream
8 to 10 macadamia nuts, coarsely chopped

Process the cookies and 1/2 cup macadamia nuts in a food processor to fine crumbs. Add the butter and sugar and process until mixed. Press over the bottom and up the side of a 9-inch pie plate. Freeze until frozen. Beat the egg yolks, sweetened condensed milk and cream cheese in a bowl. Beat in the lime juice gradually. Pour into the prepared pie crust. Top with the whipped cream. Sprinkle with the coarsely chopped macadamia nuts. Chill for 8 to 10 hours before serving.

Note: If you are concerned about using raw egg yolks, use egg yolks pasteurized in their shells, or use an equivalent amount of egg yolk substitute.

Serves 8

Pucker-Up Lemon Cranberry Pie

1 (2-crust) pie pastry
1 1/4 to 1 1/3 cups sugar
2 tablespoons all-purpose flour
3 cups fresh cranberries
2 large lemons, peeled and sliced into thin half circles
1 egg white, beaten
1 tablespoon water
Coarse sugar

Fit one of the pie pastries into a 9-inch pie plate, trimming the edge. Combine the sugar and flour in a large bowl and mix well. Add the cranberries and lemons and toss gently to coat. Spoon into the prepared pie plate. Top with the remaining pastry in a lattice design. Press the edge of the pastry lightly with a fork. Beat the egg white with the water in a small bowl. Brush over the pastry. Sprinkle with coarse sugar.

Cover the edge with foil to prevent overbrowning. Bake at 375 degrees for 25 minutes. Remove the foil and bake for 30 to 35 minutes longer or until the top is golden brown and the filling is bubbly. Cool on a wire rack.

Serves 8 to 10

Pineapple Refrigerator Pie

12 ounces whipped topping
1 (14-ounce) can sweetened condensed milk
1 large can crushed pineapple, drained
$1/4$ cup lemon juice
2 (9-inch) graham cracker pie crusts

Beat the whipped topping and sweetened condensed milk in a bowl until slightly thickened. Stir in the lemon juice. Stir in the pineapple. Spoon evenly into the pie crusts. Sprinkle with any extra crust crumbs.

Note: You may also make a graham cracker crust and press over the bottom of a 9x13-inch baking dish. Top with the filling and sprinkle with any extra crust crumbs.

Serves 8

Yummy Apple Dumplings

1¹/2 cups sugar
1 teaspoon cinnamon
2 large Granny Smith apples, peeled and cored
2 (8-count) cans refrigerator crescent roll dough
¹/2 cup (1 stick) butter, melted
1 (12-ounce) can citrus soda

Combine the sugar and cinnamon in a bowl and mix well. Cut each apple into 8 wedges and sprinkle with some of the cinnamon-sugar. Separate the crescent roll dough into triangles. Wrap each apple wedge with a dough triangle, starting at the small end and pinching the edges to seal. Arrange in a greased 9×13-inch baking dish. Sprinkle the remaining cinnamon-sugar over the dumplings. Pour the butter, then the soda over the top. Bake at 350 degrees for 35 to 45 minutes or until golden brown. Serve warm with vanilla ice cream.

Serves 8

Cream Puff Dessert

Puff Pastry
1 cup water
1/2 cup (1 stick) butter
1 cup all-purpose flour
4 eggs

Chocolate Filling
8 ounces cream cheese, softened
3 1/2 cups milk
2 (3-ounce) packages chocolate instant pudding mix

Topping
8 ounces whipped topping
1/4 cup chocolate ice cream topping
1/4 cup caramel ice cream topping
1/3 cup slivered almonds (optional)

For the pastry, combine the water and butter in a saucepan and bring to a boil over medium heat. Remove from the heat. Add the flour all at once and stir until a smooth soft dough forms. Let stand for 5 minutes. Add the eggs one at a time, beating well after each addition. Beat until smooth. Spread the dough in a greased 9×13-inch baking dish. Bake at 400 degrees for 30 to 35 minutes or until puffed and golden brown. Cool completely in the pan on a wire rack.

For the filling, beat the cream cheese, milk and pudding mix in a bowl until blended and smooth. Spread over the cooled pastry. Chill for 20 minutes.

For the topping, spread the whipped topping over the filling. Drizzle with the ice cream toppings and sprinkle with the almonds. Store any leftovers in the refrigerator.

Serves 8 to 10

Oreo Ice Cream Dessert

20 chocolate sandwich cookies, crumbled
1/2 cup (1 stick) butter
1 (6-ounce) package chocolate chips
3 eggs, beaten
2 cups confectioners' sugar
1/4 cup crème de menthe
1/2 gallon vanilla ice cream, slightly softened

Reserve 1 tablespoon of the cookie crumbs for the topping. Spread the remaining cookie crumbs over the bottom of a 9×13-inch freezer-safe dish.

Heat the butter and chocolate chips in a large bowl in the microwave until melted, stirring after 1 minute to blend. Beat the eggs with the confectioners' sugar in a bowl. Add to the chocolate mixture and mix until smooth. Pour over the cookie layer. Freeze for 1 hour.

Stir the crème de menthe into the ice cream. Spoon over the frozen layers and sprinkle with the reserved 1 tablespoon cookie crumbs. Freeze for 8 to 10 hours. Slice to serve.

Serves 15

Pecan Pie Bread Pudding

8 cups bite-size bread pieces
2 tablespoons unsalted butter, melted
3 eggs
1 1/4 cups light corn syrup
1/3 cup packed light brown sugar
1/4 cup granulated sugar
1 teaspoon maple or vanilla extract
1 teaspoon cinnamon
1/2 teaspoon salt
1 cup pecans, chopped or halved

Line an 8×8-inch baking dish with baking parchment and coat well with nonstick cooking spray. Arrange the bread in the prepared dish. Drizzle with the butter. Whisk the eggs, corn syrup, brown sugar, granulated sugar, maple extract, cinnamon and salt together in a large bowl. Stir in the pecans. Pour evenly over the bread. Move the bread around in the baking dish using a rubber spatula to coat well. Bake at 375 degrees for 45 minutes. Serve warm.

Serves 4 to 6

Praline Cheesecake

Graham Cracker Crust
1 cup graham cracker crumbs
1/4 cup sugar
4 to 6 tablespoons unsalted butter, melted

Filling
48 ounces cream cheese, softened
2 cups packed dark brown sugar (about 1 pound)
1/4 cup all-purpose flour
6 eggs
4 teaspoons vanilla extract
2/3 cup chopped pecans

For the crust, grease a 10-inch springform pan and line with baking parchment. Place the pan in the center of two large pieces of foil and wrap the bottom of the pan and partway up the side with foil. Combine the graham cracker crumbs, sugar and butter in a bowl and mix well. Press over the bottom of the prepared pan.

For the filling, beat the cream cheese with the brown sugar and flour in a large bowl until blended and smooth. Add the eggs and vanilla and mix well. Pour into the prepared crust, smoothing the top. Sprinkle with the pecans. Place the springform pan in a larger baking pan. Pour enough water into the larger pan to reach halfway up the side of the springform pan. Bake at 300 degrees for 11/2 hours or until slightly firm to the touch.

Serves 12

Pumpkin Pie Dessert Squares

1 (2-layer) package yellow cake mix
1/2 cup (1 stick) margarine, melted
1 egg
3 cups pumpkin pie filling
2 eggs
3/4 cup evaporated milk
1/4 cup sugar
1 teaspoon cinnamon
1/4 cup (1/2 stick) margarine, softened

Reserve 1 cup of the cake mix for the topping. Combine the remaining cake mix with 1/2 cup melted margarine and 1 egg in a bowl and mix well. Press over the bottom of a greased 9×13-inch baking dish. Beat the pie filling, 2 eggs and evaporated milk in a bowl until blended. Pour over the crust. Combine the reserved 1 cup cake mix with the sugar, cinnamon and 1/4 cup margarine in a bowl and mix until crumbly. Sprinkle over the prepared layers. Bake at 350 degrees for 50 minutes. Let cool before serving.

Serves 12

Pumpkin Roll

Cream Cheese Filling

8 ounces cream cheese, softened
1 cup confectioners' sugar

2 tablespoons butter, softened
1 1/2 teaspoons vanilla extract

Pumpkin Cake

2/3 cup pumpkin purée
3 eggs
1 cup sugar

3/4 cup all-purpose flour
1 teaspoon baking soda
1 teaspoon cinnamon

For the filling, beat the cream cheese, confectioners' sugar, butter and vanilla in a bowl until smooth and blended.

For the cake, grease a 10×15-inch cake pan and line with waxed paper. Combine the pumpkin, eggs and sugar in a bowl and beat well. Beat in the flour, baking soda and cinnamon just until blended. Pour into the prepared pan.

Bake at 350 degrees for 18 minutes. Invert the cake onto a kitchen towel dusted with confectioners' sugar and remove the waxed paper. Roll as for a jelly roll, using the towel to wrap tightly. Let cool.

Unroll the cake from the towel and spread Cream Cheese Filling evenly over the cake. Roll up to enclose the filling. Chill, wrapped in foil, until serving time.

Note: The Pumpkin Roll may be made in advance and frozen. After assembling, wrap in waxed paper, then wrap tightly with foil. Freeze until needed. Let thaw before slicing.

Serves 8 to 10

Rhubarb Crunch

Oat Topping

1 cup all-purpose flour
1 cup packed brown sugar
3/4 cup rolled oats

1 teaspoon cinnamon
1/2 cup (1 stick) margarine,
melted

Rhubarb

1 cup sugar
2 tablespoons cornstarch
1 cup water
1 teaspoon vanilla extract

1 or 2 drops red food coloring
(optional)
4 cups chopped rhubarb

For the topping, combine the flour, brown sugar, oats and cinnamon in a bowl and mix well. Add the margarine and mix until crumbly.

For the rhubarb, combine the sugar and cornstarch in a saucepan. Whisk in the water. Cook over medium heat until thickened and clear, stirring frequently. Remove from the heat and stir in the vanilla and food coloring.

Press half the Oat Topping over the bottom of an ungreased 9×13-inch baking dish. Spread the rhubarb over the crust. Pour the sauce evenly over the rhubarb, then top with the remaining Oat Topping. Bake at 350 degrees for 1 hour.

Serve with whipped cream or vanilla ice cream.

Note: Make Strawberry Rhubarb Crunch by preparing as above, substituting 2 cups sliced strawberries for 2 cups of the rhubarb.

Serves 8 to 10

Strawberry Pretzel Dessert

1/2 cup (1 stick) butter
1/4 cup sugar
2 cups crushed thin pretzels
8 ounces cream cheese, softened
8 ounces whipped topping
1 cup sugar
2 small packages strawberry gelatin
2 cups boiling water
2 (10-ounce) packages frozen sliced strawberries
1 (20-ounce) can crushed pineapple, drained (optional)

Melt the butter in a saucepan over low to medium heat. Stir in 1/4 cup sugar until dissolved. Stir in the crushed pretzels until well coated. Spread evenly over the bottom of a 9×13-inch baking dish, trying not to leave any gaps. Bake at 325 degrees for 5 to 10 minutes. Let cool.

Beat the cream cheese, whipped topping and 1 cup sugar in a bowl until blended and smooth. Spread evenly over the pretzel crust. Chill in the refrigerator.

Dissolve the gelatin in the boiling water in a large heatproof bowl. Heat the strawberries just until warm and stir into the gelatin mixture. Stir in the pineapple. Chill until partially set.

Spoon evenly over the cream cheese layer. Chill for 8 to 10 hours before serving.

Serves 12

Holiday Cherry Cheese Bars

Coconut Crust

1 1/4 cups all-purpose flour
1/2 cup packed brown sugar
1/2 cup butter flavor shortening,
or 1/2 cup (1 stick) butter
1/2 cup walnuts, finely chopped
1/2 cup flaked coconut

Filling

16 ounces cream cheese,
softened
2/3 cup sugar
2 eggs
2 teaspoons vanilla extract

1 (21-ounce) can cherry
pie filling
1/2 cup walnuts, coarsely
chopped

For the crust, combine the flour and brown sugar in a bowl. Cut in the shortening until fine crumbs form. Add the walnuts and coconut and mix well. Reserve 1/2 cup of the crust mixture. Press the remaining crust mixture over the bottom of a greased 9×13-inch baking dish. Bake at 350 degrees for 12 to 15 minutes or until the edges are light brown. Maintain the oven temperature.

For the filling, beat the cream cheese, sugar, eggs and vanilla in a bowl until smooth and blended. Spread over the hot baked crust. Bake for 15 minutes. Remove from the oven. Maintain the oven temperature. Spread the pie filling over the cream cheese layer. Combine the walnuts with the reserved 1/2 cup crust mixture. Sprinkle evenly over the pie filling. Bake for 15 minutes. Let cool completely. Chill for several hours. Cut into bars to serve.

Note: These bars are also excellent with blueberry pie filling in place of the cherry pie filling.

Makes about 26

Alice's Chocolate Kiss Peanut Butter Cookies

2 2/3 cups sifted all-purpose flour
2 teaspoons baking soda
1 teaspoon salt
1 cup (2 sticks) butter, softened
2/3 cup peanut butter
1 cup packed brown sugar
1 cup granulated sugar
2 eggs
2 teaspoons vanilla extract
Additional granulated sugar
48 chocolate kisses candies, unwrapped

Sift the flour, baking soda and salt together. Beat the butter and peanut butter in a bowl until well blended. Beat in the brown sugar and 1 cup granulated sugar until light and fluffy. Add the eggs and vanilla and beat until smooth. Add the dry ingredients and mix well.

Shape the dough into balls 1 tablespoon at a time. Roll in granulated sugar to coat. Arrange 2 inches apart on an ungreased cookie sheet. Bake at 375 degrees for 8 minutes.

Remove from the oven and press a candy onto the center of each cookie. Bake for 2 minutes longer. Cool on the cookie sheet for several minutes. Remove to a wire rack to cool completely.

Makes 4 dozen

Maxine's Potato Chip Cookies

1/2 cup (1 stick) butter, softened
1/2 cup (1 stick) margarine, softened
1 1/2 cups all-purpose flour

1/2 cup sugar
1 teaspoon vanilla extract
3/4 cup crushed potato chips

Beat the butter and margarine in a bowl until light and fluffy. Add the flour, sugar and vanilla and beat until blended. Stir in the potato chips using a large spoon. Drop by teaspoonfuls onto an ungreased cookie sheet. Bake at 325 degrees for 15 to 18 minutes; do not allow to brown.

Makes 4 dozen

Sweet and Salty Treats

36 pecan halves
36 small square salted pretzels
36 chocolate-covered caramel candies,
unwrapped (Rolo brand preferred)

Arrange the pecans in a single layer on a baking sheet lightly coated with nonstick cooking spray. Bake at 350 degrees for about 5 minutes or until lightly toasted. Maintain the oven temperature. Remove to a plate to cool. Arrange the pretzels in a single layer on the baking sheet. Place one candy on each pretzel. Bake for 4 to 5 minutes or just until the candies start to soften. Remove from the oven. Top each candy with a toasted pecan half. Let cool for about 10 minutes.

Makes 3 dozen

Recipe Contributors

Alice Collins
Alice Whitney
Anne Daniels
Barbara Paget
Bea Ritchey
Beth Appleton
Beth Hoopes
Betty Lou Douglas
Beverly Guthrie
Bill Short
Bud Hayes
Carla Mulcay
Cathy Browne
Celeste Crews
Charlotte Bacher
Cindy Clark
Connie Dehner
Diane Fitzell
Diane Lindsay
Dina Fogleman
Dollie Cassel
Dolores Gallagher
Donna Dunkin
Dr. Gordon Sumner, Ph.D.
    Colonel, USA, Rtd.
Fran Edwards
Frances Waters
Gail M. Riegelmayer

Hal Denton
Helen Griffin
Helen Spohrer
Jennifer Lasting
Jerry Thompson
Jody Plummer
John B. Spohrer, Jr.
John Worthey
Johnny Fincher
Joyce Estes
Juanita Sigmon
Judi Little
Judy Brekke
Julie McCall
Karen Kembro
Karen Rankin
Karen Thompson
Kathy Olander
Lana Heady
Linda Rafuse
Linda Russell
Lisa Simmons
Lisle Millard
Lynda Benecick
Lynn Cassady
Mandi Singer
Margret Durso
Marilyn L. Bean

Martha Ann Dail
Martha Resotko
Mary Frances Willock
Mary Lou Short
Meghan Harris
Michelle Hicks
Nancy Budinoff
Nancy Stallard
Pam Vest
Pearle Wood
Penny Wilkens
Philip Gillaspy
Richard Watson
Sandy Gillum
Sandy Mitchem
Sharon Hutchinson
Shelley Shepard
Sherry O'Neal
Sue Genter
Sue Shadel
Susan Ficklen
Susan Kearney
Susie Stanton
Sylvia Bowman
Sylvia Rodes
Ticia Lipscomb
Verna Dekle
Virginia Glass

Index

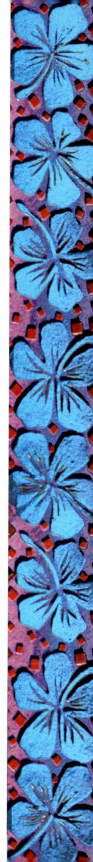

A Taste of St. George Island

The Art of Gulf Coast Cooking

St. George Island Cookbook
P.O. Box 589
St. George Island, Florida 32328
Phone: 850-927-3100
Fax: 850-927-2360
www.stgeorgeislandcookbook.com

Your Order	Quantity	Total
A Taste of St. George Island at $26.95 per book		
Postage and handling at $5.00 per book		
	Total	

Please make check payable to St. George Island Cookbook

Name

Street Address

City   State   Zip

Telephone

Photocopies will be accepted

176